# GARLIC Garlic Garlic

**Recipe ideas using the world's supreme herb**

# GARLIC Garlic *Garlic*

**Recipe ideas using the world's
supreme herb**

**Edited by Lydia Darbyshire**

Select Editions
Vancouver

Published in 2004 by **Select Publications**
3918 Kitchener Street
Burnaby BC V5C 3M2·
604-415-2444
604-415-3444

A QUINTET BOOK

ISBN 1-894905-36-9

This book was designed and produced by
Quintet Publishing Limited
6 Blundell Street
London N7 9BH

Creative Director: Richard Dewing
Art Director: Clare Reynolds
Design: Giles Ellis
Project Editor: Toria Leitch
Editor: Lydia Darbyshire
Illustrator: Shona Cameron

Material in this book previously appeared in: *The Great Chile
Pepper Cookbook*, Gina Steer; *The Real Chile Bookbook*, Marjie
Lambert; *Korean Cooking*, Hilaire Walden; *Mexican Cooking*,
Roger Hicks; *Indian Low-Fat Cooking*, Roshi Razzaq; *Thai
Cooking*, Kurt Kahrs; *Stir-Fry Cooking*, Bridget Jones; *Creole
Cooking*, Sue Mullen; *The Great Garlic Cookbook*, Sophie Hale;
*Pickles, Relishes & Chutneys*, Gail Duff; *Mexican Main Dishes*,
Marlena Spieler

Typeset in Great Britain by
Central Southern Typesetters, Eastbourne
Manufactured in Hong Kong by
Regent Publishing Pte Ltd
Printed in China by SNP
Leefung Printers Ltd

The Publisher wishes to thank the following
for permission to reproduce the illustrations:
p. 7 and 9 Casecross Ltd; p. 8 ET Archive Ltd.

# CONTENTS

# INTRODUCTION

Garlic has always been more than just a flavouring. In the course of its long history it has been worshipped by the Greeks and the Egyptians; it inspired the first recorded industrial strike; it has had binding oaths sworn upon it; it has been used as hard currency, to ward off the plague and the evil eye, and to diagnose pregnancy; and it was reputed to cure anything from cancer to thinning hair. It has also been used to preserve meats and corpses, to temper

steel, to provide vigour on the battlefield and in bed, and to keep pests from crops and vampires from virgins.

Without doubt, garlic (*Allium sativum*) is one of the most versatile plants there is. Its botanical name derives from the Latin word *allium*, which means odorous, and it is one of more than 300 species within a genus that includes onions, leeks, spring onions, shallots and chives. The word garlic itself derives from two Scandinavian or Norse words, *gar,* meaning spear, and *leac,* meaning a leek, which are clearly references to the plant's tall, slender stalk.

Most people would regard garlic as the strongest tasting vegetable, certainly the strongest of the entire onion family, with its sulfureous, pungent taste. However, that need not be the case, for, cooked carefully, the effect can be as powerful or as subtle as you wish. The quantities recommended in the recipes in this book, therefore, are not necessarily reflected in the strength of the final result. A chicken stuffed with 40 cloves of whole, blanched garlic and baked in a low oven will not be nearly as garlicky as a chicken served with an aioli (raw garlic sauce) made with an eighth of that quantity.

Some people are afraid of smelling of garlic. Parsley, chlorophyll preparations, absorbents such as peas and beans, and other breath fresheners will help. But why worry? Garlic smells like good food; bad breath is bad breath.

Garlic can be rubbed around a salad bowl or fondue pan, or crushed or finely chopped and fried over a high heat to give a strong flavour to sauces for pasta and grains.

## GARLIC IN THE KITCHEN

When you buy garlic, make sure that the bulbs are firm and well filled out, and that there are no tears in the outer sheath. The skin of the bulb can be papery white, pink or purplish, depending on where it was grown and at what time of year you buy it. But the flavour will vary little. If you want to keep it, store it in a cool, dry place.

A garlic press is useful if you use garlic a lot. Plastic is best, although you can use a stainless steel or even a wooden one. Bruise the clove lightly to loosen the skin, then crush it, unpeeled, collecting the juice and pulp as it comes through the holes. This makes cleaning the press a lot simpler: just pick out the skin and rinse the press in hot running water.

As the smell of garlic tends to linger, it is a good idea to keep a chopping board specifically for garlic and onions, and to wrap garlicky food in an airtight bag and greaseproof paper before placing it in the refrigerator or freezer.

## GARLIC IN THE GARDEN

Although garlic can be bought all year round, it is easy to grow. It is hardy, but does need a period of heat and sun while it matures. To plant, carefully separate the cloves in a garlic bulb and plant them, except the two or three in the centre 4 cm/1½ inches deep and about 15 cm/6 inches apart, pointed end up. If you are planting a lot of garlic, leave about 30 cm/12 inches between the rows. The soil should be fertile but fine and well drained. Planted in early spring, the garlic will be ready to harvest in the autumn, when the foliage will have turned brown and started to shrivel. If the bulbs are planted in mid-autumn, the garlic will be ready the following summer. Loosen the earth around each bulb with a fork, and be careful not to tear open the sheaths when you lift out the bulbs. Dry the garlic off in the sun or in an open shed, and shake off any loose soil. The bulbs can be strung together and stored in cool, dry conditions until they are needed.

Garlic can also be grown in pots on a sunny windowsill. Plant the bulbs at a depth of 2.5 cm/1 inch. Pots kept indoors near a source of heat should be well watered from the bottom.

You can also grow garlic from seed. Several varieties can be bought from seed suppliers and garden nurseries, and the seed supplier will be able to advise you on the best type to choose and the best way to cultivate it.

## GARLIC IN HISTORY

The smell of garlic has permeated history for at least 6000 years, and even longer if you take the Moslem view that when a triumphant Satan left the Garden of Eden, onions sprang from his right footprint and garlic from his left. Garlic is believed to have originated in the Siberian desert, been brought to Egypt by way of Asian nomadic tribes, and from there back up through India via the trade routes to eastern Asia, then west to Europe. It was carried by Phoenician traders and Viking sailors, who believed it would fortify

(left) Garlic chives growing.

(right) The Indian woman is using a large sieve to separate the garlic cloves from the loose outer skins.

them on their journeys and help them to treat any illnesses that struck on the voyage.

For all these cultures, whether Indian or Egyptian, Babylonian, Greek, Russian, Hebrew or Chinese, garlic was almost as important an element of their daily lives as salt. Had the Roman ruling classes been less snobbish about the pungency, we might now be receiving an "alliary" instead of the (salt-derived) salary. In ancient Egypt, 15 pounds would buy a slave, and, until the middle of the eighteenth century, the Siberians paid their taxes in garlic.

*A fourteenth-century illustration shows how important garlic was medicinally at this time, even if its culinary use was limited.*

By the time of Horace (65–8 BC), garlic was frowned on by upper class Roman households, although it was consumed by the mass of people in great quantities. Garlic was especially popular with the army, who planted it wherever they went, and it soon became a symbol of military life.

Marco Polo (1254–1324) recorded that the Chinese used garlic to preserve raw meat and to detoxify – and disguise the taste of – any meat that had gone off. The Egyptians used it as part of the mummification process and buried it with the dead. Six cloves of garlic were found in Tutankhamen's tomb, while painted clay models of garlic bulbs have been discovered in pre-pharaonic burial sites, put there to ward off any evil spirits that might impede the soul's journey to the afterlife. Bodies found in Theban tombs wear necklaces of garlic for much the same reason.

Garlic's protective powers against malign spirits – especially the evil eye – also applied to the living. In modern Egypt there is still a festival known as 'sniffing the breezes' during which garlic is eaten, worn, and smashed on doorframes and windowsills to keep malignant forces at bay.

Wherever it was popular, garlic was a class indicator, soon spurned by the upwardly mobile, the aristocracy and, in some cases, by the clergy, but enthusiastically embraced as food and physic by the masses, causing the French author Raspail to call it the 'camphor of the poor'. Such snobbery could prove fatal: during an epidemic in 1608, visiting French priests could comfort London's sick with no ill-effects, due to the garlic they ate, while many of their English counterparts died.

## GARLIC IN FOLKLORE

Garlic is probably best know, outside the kitchen, as a vampire repellant. In Bram Stocker's Dracula (1897), the Dutch vampire expert Abraham Van Helsing makes Count Dracula's intended victim, Lucy, wear a wreath of garlic flowers, and he rubs them around the window, door and fireplace of her bedroom as the first line of defense.

The Saxons of Transylvania in central Europe, the very heart of vampire country, would stuff the mouths of suspect corpses with garlic before burial. A few cloves kept in a money bag were believed to keep witches from your gold and, hung in dairies, to stop supernatural interference with milk production. If you gave garlic away, however, the 'luck' would go with it.

Throughout antiquity, garlic was regarded as a protection for those vulnerable to the evil eye—virgins, newborn infants (no Greek midwife would attempt a delivery without a good supply of garlic to hand), engaged couples and newly weds. Indeed, anyone could be subject to malign influences at some time or another, and if the worst should happen and no garlic were to hand at a potentially hazardous moment, a loud cry of "Here's garlic in your eyes!" was believed to do the trick.

## GARLIC IN MEDICINE

The number of ailments and afflictions that have been treated by applications of garlic over the years is almost endless: acne, alopecia, altitude sickness, animal bites, arteriosclerosis, asthma, athlete's foot, bee stings, bronchitis, bruises, cancer, catarrh, cold symptoms, constipation, eczema, epilepsy, exhaustion, flatulence, gangrene, greying hair, gastric disorders, headaches, hypertension, hypoglycaemia, insanity, jaundice, leprosy, most poisons, obesity, open wounds, piles, poison ivy, rabies, scabies, sciatica, scurvy, senility, snakebite, toothache, tuberculosis, whooping cough and worms.

The ancient Egyptians, who were the first to practice medicine as we know it, featured many garlic-based cures in their pharmacopoeia. These were adapted by both Hippocrates (460–377 BC), known as the Father of Medicine, who recognized its value as a diuretic and a laxative, and by Dioscorides (40–90), whose medical texts were standard works until the late Middle Ages. The Chinese are believed to have used garlic medicinally since 2000 BC, while in India, the 5000-year-old system of Ayurvedic medicine, which features garlic-based cures for such ailments as heartburn, hoarseness and typhus, still flourishes.

In the Middle Ages in Europe, books emerged, packed with plant-based recipes and lore, these books combined the folk medicine of the time (such as the tying of cut garlic cloves to the soles of the feet as a cough cure) and a growing interest in and appreciation of botany and natural science, and it was at this time that the fundamental principles of what we now know as homeopathy, naturopathy and herbalism emerged. These disciplines remained popular until the end of the nineteenth century, by which time the medical mainstream had turned to the more 'scientific' methods of a newly industrial society, but they are now enjoying a resurgence and winning new supporters.

*(above) The chef with the flaming pan is cooking at the Gilroy Garlic Festival, an annual event held in Gilroy, California.*

*(left) In China, the shoots of garlic are eaten as often as the bulbs.*

*(right) Chinese men taking exercise before their morning meal which will contain herbs and garlic for health.*

# SOUPS & APPETIZERS

# ARCADIAN GARLIC SOUP

SERVES 4 ~ 6

*In 'The Passionate Shepherd To His Love,' the poet Virgil mentions 'a fragrant soup of pounded garlic and wild-thyme for the reapers wearied by the scorching heat.' This could be the sort of thing he had in mind.*

### INGREDIENTS

15–20 garlic cloves, unpeeled

5 Tbsp olive oil

1.1 litres/2 pints chicken or veal stock

2 tsp fresh thyme

½ tsp salt

freshly ground white pepper

3 egg yolks

sliced French bread or toast, to serve

grated cheese, to serve

Blanch the garlic in boiling water for 1 minute, drain and peel. Cook it, but do not let it brown, in half the oil for 10 minutes. Add the stock, thyme, salt and plenty of white pepper. Simmer for 30 minutes and check the seasoning.

Sieve or blend the soup, keeping a few garlic cloves whole. Return the soup to its saucepan and keep hot.

Beat the egg yolks and gradually add the remaining oil. Stir a couple of spoonfuls of the soup in to the egg mixture, remove the soup from the heat, and add the egg in a thin stream, stirring well.

Serve immediately with sliced French bread or toast, and a sprinkling of grated cheese in each bowl.

# GARLIC ONION SOUP

SERVES 6

## INGREDIENTS

vegetable oil for frying

1 large onion, sliced

3 garlic bulbs, finely chopped

1 Tbsp flour

½ tsp Dijon mustard

1 litre/1¾ pints vegetable stock

250 ml/8 fl oz dry white wine

salt and freshly ground black pepper

a little butter

6 slices of French bread

6 slices Gruyère cheese,
about 25 g/1 oz each

Heat the oil in a large saucepan. Add the onion and shortly after add the garlic. Keep on a low heat.

Stir in the flour, then add the Dijon mustard, stock and wine, stirring the mixture continually.

Simmer until the onion is soft, then season to taste.

Butter the bread and top each with a slice of cheese.

Pour the soup into 6 individual ovenproof dishes. Float a slice of bread on each and place under a preheated grill until the cheese is browned and bubbling. Serve immediately.

# CREAM OF GARLIC AND MUSHROOM SOUP

SERVES 3 ~ 4

*Add garlic to this classic recipe for a change.*

### INGREDIENTS

2 heads of garlic (about 25 cloves)

225 g/8 oz white button mushrooms, wiped and halved

75 g/3 oz butter

1 tsp fresh thyme

4 Tbsp plain flour

300 ml/½ pint chicken stock

300 ml/½ pint milk

6 Tbsp single cream

salt and freshly ground black pepper

2 Tbsp chopped parsley, to serve

50 g/2 oz button mushrooms, wiped and halved

Separate the garlic cloves and blanch them in boiling water for 1 minute. Drain and peel.

Sweat the mushrooms in the butter for 5 minutes. Lift them out of the pan and keep to one side.

Add the garlic and thyme to the butter and mushroom juices and gently cook with the lid on for 10–15 minutes, until the garlic cloves are just tender.

Stir in the flour and cook for several minutes. Turn up the heat and add the stock and milk, a little at a time, stirring well. Simmer the mixture for 10 minutes.

Add the mushrooms and simmer for another minute until they are heated through. Remove from the heat and stir in the cream. Season with salt and pepper to taste.

Serve sprinkled with the chopped parsley and thinly sliced crisp, raw mushrooms, for texture.

# STUFFED MUSHROOMS

SERVES 4

*Garlic goes particularly well with mushrooms. Bring back this old favourite as a tasty start to a meal.*

### INGREDIENTS

8 large, flat mushrooms

75 g/3 oz butter, softened

2–3 garlic cloves, finely chopped

2 Tbsp fresh white breadcrumbs

1 Tbsp finely chopped parsley

Wipe the mushrooms and cut off the stems, as close as possible to the caps.

Mash together the butter and garlic.

Arrange the mushrooms, gill side up, on a greased baking sheet and dot with the garlic and butter mixture. Cover with foil and bake at 350°F/180°C/gas 4 for 15–20 minutes or until the mushrooms are tender.

Remove the foil and top the mushrooms with the breadcrumbs and parsley. Grill at a high heat until the breadcrumbs are browned.

*Stuffed Mushrooms* ▶

# GREEN 'PISTOU' SOUP

### SERVES 4

*The lovely, all-green colour is an unexpected delight. Add pasta if you like, and to make
a classic pistou add a handful of cooked vermicelli to the pot.*

### INGREDIENTS

I leek, chopped

2 onions, chopped

5 garlic cloves, coarsely chopped

3 Tbsp extra-virgin olive oil

3 medium ripe, yellow tomatoes, diced

salt and freshly ground black pepper
to taste

I litre/1¾ pints vegetable stock

I litre/1¾ pints water

3 small courgettes, cut into
bite-sized pieces

I medium sized, waxy potato,
peeled and diced

¼ cabbage, thinly sliced

¾ cup fresh, white, shell beans (such as
haricot, shelled and cooked,
or cooked cannellini)

8 Swiss chard or spinach leaves,
thinly sliced

¼–½ bunch broccoli, cut into florets

handful of green beans,
cut into bite-sized pieces

I batch of pistou (page 173), to serve

extra grated Parmesan, to serve

Lightly sauté the leek, onion and garlic in the olive oil until they are soft, then add the tomatoes and cook over a medium heat for about 10 minutes. Season to taste with salt and black pepper.

Add the vegetable stock and water, the courgette, potato and cabbage, and continue to cook over a medium heat until the potatoes are just tender and the courgettes are quite soft. The cabbage will be soft by now, too.

Add the white beans, chard or spinach leaves, broccoli and green beans, and cook for about another 5 minutes, or until the broccoli and green beans are cooked through.

Serve immediately in bowls with a tablespoon or two of pistou stirred in, accompanied by grated Parmesan to taste. Do not heat the pistou, or its fragrance will dissipate.

# CREAMY PURÉE OF WHITE BEANS AND PORCINI

SERVES 4 ~ 6

*Humble beans puréed with luxurious wild mushrooms create a classic soup through the southwest of France. The soup is sometimes served with a scattering of shredded prosciutto, a shaving of truffle, a drizzle of truffle oil, or a scattering of diced foie gras.*

### INGREDIENTS

cooked white beans (such as cannellini or haricots)

2 litres/4 pints stock, preferably ham

75 g/3 oz diced ham or bacon (such as pancetta or prosciutto)

I carrot, diced

I baking potato, diced

2–3 tsp fresh thyme leaves

5 garlic cloves, roughly chopped

50 g/2 oz dried mushrooms (such as porcini)

250 ml/8 fl oz water

3 Tbsp brandy

salt and freshly ground black pepper

25 g/I oz unsalted butter or 3 Tbsp double cream

In a saucepan, combine the beans with the stock, ham or bacon, carrot, potato, half the thyme and the garlic. Bring to the boil, then reduce the heat to low, and simmer for about 30 minutes, until the vegetables are tender and cooked through.

Meanwhile, place the mushrooms with the water and brandy in a saucepan. Gradually bring to the boil, then reduce the heat, and simmer for about 15 minutes until the mushrooms are tender.

Remove the mushrooms from the liquid, chop roughly, and add them to the soup. Strain the liquid, discarding the gritty bits, and add the strained liquid to the soup.

Mix the soup in the blender or food processor until smooth. Taste for seasoning, then stir in the butter or cream. Serve immediately in warmed bowls, garnished with thyme.

# CLASSIC GREEK VEGETABLE SOUP

SERVES 6 ~ 8

*Serve this classic Greek soup with freshly baked olive bread (eliopitta).*

### INGREDIENTS

100 ml/4 fl oz olive oil

2 garlic cloves, crushed

2 onions, finely chopped

225 g/8 oz cabbage, finely shredded

3 carrots, chopped

3 celery sticks, chopped

2 large potatoes, peeled and diced

2 litres/4 pints vegetable stock or water

4 tomatoes, skinned, seeded and chopped

salt and freshly ground black pepper

4 Tbsp chopped fresh parsley

50 g/2 oz feta or kefalotyri cheese, grated

Heat the olive oil in a large saucepan and add the garlic and onion. Cook for 5 minutes, until the onion is softened but not coloured. Add the cabbage and continue to cook for another 3–4 minutes.

Add the carrots and celery to the saucepan, stir and cook for a further 5 minutes. Add the potatoes, stir and cook gently for another 5 minutes, until the vegetables are softened. Next pour in the vegetable stock or water and stir well. Increase the heat to bring the soup to the boil. Cover and simmer for 12–15 minutes. Add the tomato and season to taste with salt and freshly ground black pepper.

Re-cover the pan and gently simmer the soup for about 1 hour. Stir in the parsley just before the end of the cooking time. Serve sprinkled with grated cheese.

# FRAGRANT LETTUCE SOUP

SERVES 4 ~ 6

### INGREDIENTS

6 garlic cloves, unpeeled

2 large Romaine lettuces

3 Tbsp finely chopped onion

40 g/1½ oz butter

25 g/1 oz flour

½ tsp sugar

salt and freshly ground black pepper

900 ml/1½ pints milk or milk
and water, mixed

2 egg yolks

3 Tbsp single cream

1 Tbsp chopped fresh parsley, chives, or
mint, to serve

Baked Garlic Croutons, to serve (page 61)

Plunge the unpeeled garlic cloves into boiling water and simmer for about 8 minutes. Drain, peel and chop them coarsely.

Wash the lettuce and shred the leaves finely. Stew it gently with the onions in the butter for 5 minutes.

Stir in the parboiled garlic and cook for a further 5 minutes. Remove the vegetables from the heat and add the flour, sugar and a little salt and pepper. Return to the heat and add the milk. Bring the mixture to the boil and simmer for 15 minutes, or until the vegetables are tender.

Either sieve or blend the soup and return it to the saucepan. Check the seasoning to taste.

Combine the egg yolks and cream, stir them into the soup, and heat to just below boiling point (if boiled, the egg yolks will get stringy).

To serve, sprinkle the chopped fresh parsley, chives or mint over each bowlful and serve with Baked Garlic Croutons. For a more intense flavour, add a handful of roughly chopped watercress leaves to the stewing lettuce soup.

# FLOATING ISLAND SOUP

SERVES 6

## INGREDIENTS

225 g/8 oz fish trimmings

1 good-sized bunch of parsley

2–3 sprigs of fresh dill

900 ml/1½ pints water

1 medium onion, sliced

300 ml/½ pint white wine,
or wine and water mixed

salt and freshly ground white pepper

350 g/12 oz potatoes, peeled

1 small leek (white part only)

2 garlic cloves, unpeeled

½ Tbsp tomato purée

2 egg whites

1 Tbsp grated Parmesan cheese

1 tsp garlic juice

18 peeled prawns, to serve

In a large saucepan, simmer the fish trimmings, parsley, dill, water, onion and white wine with a little salt and pepper for 30 minutes.

Cut the potatoes into 2.5 cm/1-inch chunks, and then cut the leeks into thick slices.

Strain off the fish stock into a clean pan and add to it the potatoes, the leek, garlic and the tomato purée. Simmer for 15–20 minutes, until the potato is cooked.

Either sieve or blend the soup until smooth. Return to the saucepan and season with salt and pepper to taste. Bring slowly to the boil.

Whip the egg whites with a good pinch of salt until they are really stiff. Fold in the Parmesan cheese, garlic juice and a little white pepper.

Drop tablespoonfuls of the egg white mixture into the simmering soup and poach for about 5 minutes or until firm.

Serve immediately using 3 of the prawns for each bowl.

### COOK'S TIP

For a simpler soup, omit the egg white mixture and stir 1 tablespoon of single cream into each bowlful of soup. Serve with Baked Garlic Croutons (page 61).

# CHICKEN SOUP WITH AVOCADO, CHICKPEAS AND CHILLIES

SERVES 4 ~ 6

*The soup is said to have originated in the Mexico City suburb of Tlapan, where food vendors try to capture the appetite of the strolling diners. One soup-seller hit upon the simple combination we think of today as Tlapan: avocado, chipotle chillies, chickpeas, chicken stock and lime.*

## INGREDIENTS

3 garlic cloves, coarsely chopped

1 Tbsp olive oil

2 courgettes, cut into bite-sized pieces

½ carrot, thinly sliced

1 litre/2 pints chicken stock

400 g/14 oz cooked chickpeas

1–2 canned chipotle or other hot chillies, cut into strips, plus a little of the marinade

2 spring onions, thinly sliced

about 225 g/8 oz shredded chicken

1 avocado, peeled, stoned and diced

1 Tbsp chopped fresh coriander

handful of tortilla chips, preferably low-salt ones

1 lime, cut into wedges

Warm the garlic in the olive oil without browning. Add the courgettes, carrot, chicken stock and chickpeas, then bring to the boil. Reduce the heat and simmer for about 10 minutes or until the vegetables are tender.

Ladle the soup into bowls and garnish each with a little chipotle, spring onions, shredded chicken, avocado, coriander, tortilla chips and wedges of lime.

### COOK'S TIP
Canned chipotles are very hot, red chillies with a strong smoky taste. They are available in specialist shops, otherwise substitute other bottled chillies, with a dash of Tabasco and hickory smoke flavouring.

# BEEF, AUBERGINE AND GREEN PEPPER SOUP

SERVES 4 ~ 6

*A spicy broth or soup with the flavours of the Pacific Rim. Serve this as a lunch or supper dish with bread,*
*or add a spoonful of cooked rice to each helping to make more substantial a dish.*

### INGREDIENTS

100 g/4 oz boneless chuck steak

3 Tbsp peanut oil

1 large onion, finely chopped

4 garlic cloves, finely chopped

1 small aubergine, finely diced

1 hot red chilli, seeded and
very finely chopped

1 green pepper, cored, deseeded and
finely sliced

2.5 cm/1–inch piece fresh ginger, peeled
and finely sliced

1 stick lemon grass, bruised
and finely chopped

3 fresh lime leaves, finely shredded
(use dried if fresh are not available)

1.1 litres/2 pints well-flavoured stock

soya sauce, to taste

salt, to taste

Cut the beef into 1 cm/½-inch strips, then slice it very finely. Heat the oil in a large pan, add the beef and cook quickly until well browned. Add the onion, garlic, aubergine, chilli, pepper, ginger and lemon grass, then cover the pan and cook slowly for 4–5 minutes.

Add the lime leaves and stock, then bring to the boil. Cover and simmer for at least 1 hour, until all the ingredients are tender and the flavours have blended together.

Season the soup to taste with soya sauce and salt. Serve with crusty bread or rice if you wish.

# COUNTRYSIDE SOUP OF MUSHROOMS AND GREEN LENTILS

SERVES 4 ~ 6

*Serve a bowlful of this soup on a cold winter's day accompanied by crusty wholemeal bread and some soured cream to spoon into the soup.*

### INGREDIENTS

100 g/4 oz green lentils

3 bay leaves

750 ml/1¼ pints water

750 ml/1¼ pints stock

2–3 potatoes, peeled and diced

1 carrot, chopped

275 g/10 oz flat black mushrooms, diced

5 garlic cloves, chopped

3 Tbsp olive oil

salt and freshly ground
black pepper, to taste

1–2 tsp chopped fresh thyme or savory

Combine the green lentils with the bay leaves and water in a saucepan. Bring to the boil, reduce the heat to low, and cook, covered, until the lentils are just tender but not falling apart. Remove the bay leaves.

Add the stock, potatoes and carrot, and cook over medium heat.

Meanwhile, fry the mushrooms with the garlic in the olive oil. Season with salt and pepper. When the potatoes are cooked through and beginning to fall apart, add the cooked mushrooms to the soup, along with the thyme or savory.

Continue to cook for 15–20 minutes more, crushing the potatoes as you stir. Taste, adjust the seasoning if necessary, and serve hot.

### COOK'S TIP

The best and most flavoursome stock is always homemade. Fresh stock is now widely available in supermarkets. Stock cubes may be used at a pinch, unless the recipe states otherwise.

# BOUILLABAISSE

### SERVES 8

*Variations on this substantial soup—almost a fish stew—abound all over the Mediterranean,
the only constant being to use as many different types of fish as you can.*

### INGREDIENTS

1.25 kg/2½ lb fish

225 g/8 oz shellfish

4 Tbsp olive oil

1 large onion, coarsely chopped

4 garlic cloves, crushed

450 ml/¾ pint white wine

1 Tbsp fresh mixed herbs

pinch of saffron threads (optional)

350 g/12 oz tomatoes, skinned, seeded
and coarsely chopped

1 tsp sugar

salt and freshly ground white pepper

a little cayenne

16 slices of French bread fried in oil or
Clarified Garlic Butter (page 180)

Clean the fish and cut it into equal-sized pieces. Small fish can be left whole. Scrub any mussels or clams, and beard the mussels. Shell any prawns and, if using scallops, cut the meat out of the shell and halve.

Separate the fish onto three plates, one for firm-fleshed fish and one for soft-fleshed varieties. Keep any squid on a separate plate.

Heat the oil in a large saucepan and fry the onion until it begins to brown. Add the garlic and cook for several minutes. Add the wine, mixed herbs and saffron, if used.

Simmer for 5 minutes, add any squid and cook for 10 minutes.

Add the firm-fleshed fish and cook for 10 more minutes. Add the soft-fleshed fish and simmer until almost cooked. You may need to add some water so that the liquid still covers the fish.

Add the tomatoes, prepared shellfish and sugar, and season with salt, pepper and a little cayenne. Cook for a further 5 minutes, by which time any clams or mussels will have opened up.

Serve with the fried bread and a good dollop of Aïoli (page 171) in each bowl.

# BASQUE WILD MUSHROOM SOUP

SERVES 4

*The flavours of wild mushrooms and chorizo combine deliciously in this highly flavoured and robust soup,*
*which is surprisingly light, and suitable for the summer or warm weather in the fall.*

### INGREDIENTS

25 g/1 oz mixed exotic mushrooms (such
as trompette de la mort, mousserons and
morels), including a few slices of dried
porcini or 25 g/1 oz porcini

450 ml/¾ pint water

1 onion, chopped

4 garlic cloves, roughly chopped

2 Tbsp olive oil

225 g/8 oz drained, cooked, chickpeas

450 ml/¾ pint chicken stock

¼–½ tsp chopped fresh rosemary

75 g/3 oz Spanish chorizo sausage, cut
into julienne strips

salt and freshly ground
black pepper, to taste

Place the mushrooms in a large saucepan with the water, and bring to the boil. Remove from the heat and leave to rehydrate for about 15 minutes. Squeeze out the mushrooms, letting all of the liquid drip back into the pan.

Chop the mushrooms, strain the liquid, and set both aside.

Lightly fry the onion and garlic in the olive oil. Add the chickpeas and cook for a few moments more, then add the strained mushroom liquid, and bring to the boil.

Take about a quarter of the chickpea mixture and mix in a blender or food processor until it is smooth. Add a little more liquid from the saucepan if necessary. Return the mixture to the saucepan, along with the mushrooms, stock, rosemary and chorizo. Bring to the boil, reduce the heat, and simmer for a few minutes until warmed through.

Taste for seasoning, and add more salt and pepper if necessary. Serve the soup immediately.

### COOK'S TIP

For a quick soup, use canned rather than dried chickpeas. The result will be just as good.

# GANOUG GANOUG

SERVES 4

### INGREDIENTS

2 aubergines

2–3 garlic cloves, finely crushed

2 Tbsp olive oil

1 Tbsp lemon juice

salt and freshly ground black pepper

Wrap the aubergines in oiled kitchen foil, place on a baking sheet, and bake for 30–45 minutes or until soft.

Split open the aubergines and scoop out the pulp. Mash the pulp with the garlic, oil and lemon juice. Season with salt and pepper to taste, and chill.

Serve very cold with warm, dry toast and chilled fresh butter.

# TOMATO AND GREEN PEPPER GAZPACHO

### SERVES 4

*The creaminess of this thick soup comes from the puréed stale bread and olive oil, which are blended with the vegetables. It is a specialty of Andalusia and is traditionally made by pounding, although a blender works just as well. Serve with a crisp garnish.*

### INGREDIENTS

100 g/4 oz stale white bread

175 ml/6 fl oz extra-virgin olive oil

350 g/12 oz ripe tomatoes, diced

1 green pepper, diced

4 garlic cloves, finely chopped

2 Tbsp sherry vinegar

salt, to taste

### GARNISHES

1 hard-boiled egg, chopped

1 slice white bread, cut into cubes and browned in olive oil

1–2 slices Serrano or Parma ham, cut into thin strips

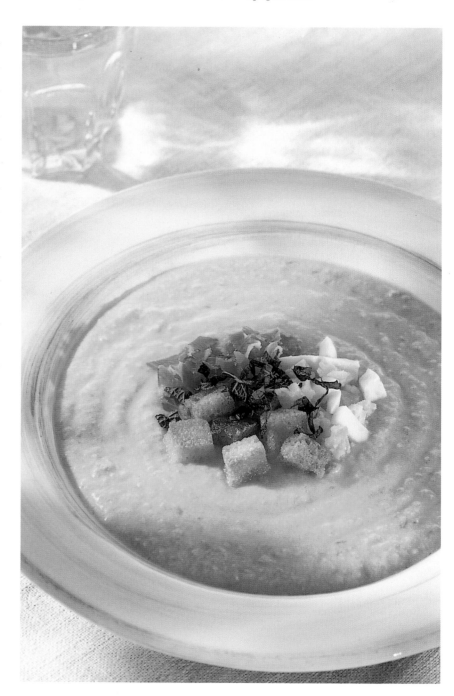

Cut or break the bread into bite-sized pieces. Place them in the food processor or blender, pour over cold water to cover and leave for a moment or two. Drain.

Add the olive oil, tomatoes, green pepper, garlic, sherry vinegar and salt. Blend until a thick purée forms. Season to taste and chill until ready to serve with the optional garnishes.

# AUBERGINE GUACAMOLE

SERVES 4 ~ 6

*For all diet-conscious lovers of Mexican food! This is a low-calorie version of the*
*traditional avocado dip.*

### INGREDIENTS

I large aubergine

I avocado, peeled and finely chopped

grated rind and juice of I lime

2 tomatoes, seeded and finely chopped

I green chilli, seeded and
very finely chopped

I Tbsp very finely chopped onion

I–2 garlic cloves, crushed

salt and freshly ground black pepper

olive oil, to drizzle

paprika, to sprinkle

Preheat the oven to 425°F/220°C/ gas 7. Prick the aubergine all over, then place it on a baking sheet and roast for 30–40 minutes, until wrinkled and tender. Cover with a damp cloth and leave to cool completely.

Peel the aubergine, then chop the flesh into small pieces. Blend to a fairly smooth paste in a blender or food processor, then turn into a small bowl.

Toss the avocado in the lime juice, then add to the aubergine with the remaining ingredients. Stir the mixture carefully until well combined. Season generously with salt and pepper, then drizzle with a little olive oil and sprinkle with paprika.

Serve the guacamole with tortilla chips or warm toast.

# ROASTED TOMATOES WITH OLIVE OIL, GARLIC AND BASIL

SERVES 4

*Serve with crusty bread to soak up the juices and tomato. Capers, olives or anchovies can be scattered on top, for a salty Mediterranean flavour.*

### INGREDIENTS

12 small to medium sized ripe, flavourful tomatoes

4–5 Tbsp extra-virgin olive oil

½–1 tsp balsamic vinegar, or to taste

coarse sea salt, to taste

3–5 garlic cloves, finely chopped

handful of fresh basil, coarsely torn

Arrange the tomatoes in a casserole, spaced apart, and drizzle lightly with a little of the olive oil (1–2 teaspoons).

Preheat the oven to 425°F/220°C/gas 7. Place the tomatoes in the oven and roast for 20 minutes, then reduce the heat to 325°F/170°C/gas 3 and cook for a further 30 minutes. The tomato skins should be darkened and cracked, to the point of peeling off.

Remove from the oven and allow to cool, preferably overnight when the juices will thicken.

Remove the skins of the tomatoes and squeeze them, letting the juices run back onto the tomatoes.

Serve at room temperature, drizzled with olive oil, balsamic vinegar, and sprinkled with salt, garlic and basil.

# SNAIL BUNS

SERVES 4

*For many people, the high point of the snail-eating experience is mopping up the aromatic juices with fresh bread. Served this way, the juices are absorbed by the bread during cooking, which is then eaten as a* bonne bouche. *The bun tops can be used for dipping.*

### INGREDIENTS

4 large soft white rolls

3–4 garlic cloves, crushed

100 g/4 oz butter, softened

1 Tbsp chopped spring onions (green part only)

1 Tbsp chopped parsley

salt and freshly ground black pepper

16 canned snails with shells

Cut the top third off each roll and scoop out four depressions, each large enough to hold a snail shell.

Mash the garlic with the softened butter, spring onions and parsley, and season with salt and pepper.

Drain the snails and put each into its shell. Fill the shells with the garlic and butter mixture.

Put 4 stuffed snail shells into each bun, keeping them as upright as possible. Arrange them on a baking sheet and cook at 425°F/220°C/gas 7 for about 7 minutes or until the butter has melted and the snails are heated through.

Cover the filled buns with their tops, warm through to serve.

# TARAMASALATA

SERVES 4

*The only thing this delicate creation has in common with the salty, pink, commercially produced taramasalata is the name. This version is only worth making if you can get* fresh *smoked cod roe, dark red and veined on the outside and reddish-pink inside. Cod roe in tins or jars is always very salty.*

### INGREDIENTS

50 g/2 oz slice of crustless white bread

225 g/8 oz fresh smoked cod roe

2 garlic cloves, crushed

6 Tbsp olive oil

lemon juice to taste

I lemon cut into wedges, to serve

pitta bread, to serve

Soak the bread in water and squeeze it out.
Skin the roe and mash it together with the bread and garlic.

Gradually stir in the olive oil, adding lemon juice to taste.

Serve with lemon wedges and Greek pitta bread, or as a topping for baked potatoes.

### COOK'S TIP

Taramasalata can also be made in a blender, although the texture will be much lighter and thicker, and you will need to thin the mixture with a little single cream or extra lemon juice.

# TARTE MARIE-ODILE

SERVES 4 ~ 6

*Slice this tart into thin wedges and serve on its own as an appetizer.*

### INGREDIENTS

175 g/6 oz plain flour

pinch of salt

1 tsp paprika

2 pinches of cayenne

100 g/4 oz butter, softened

1 Tbsp Parmesan cheese

1 egg yolk

900 g/2 lb Ratatouille (page 145), leaving out the basil and feta

3 Tbsp soured cream

1 Tbsp coarsely chopped parsley

Sieve together the flour, salt, paprika and cayenne. Rub in the softened butter until the mixture resembles fine breadcrumbs.

Add the Parmesan and egg yolk and, if the pastry seems too stiff and crumbly, add a little cold water.

Press the pastry into a shallow cake tin or a 22-cm/9-inch pie plate. Cover with foil and baking beans and bake at 400°F/200°C/gas 6 for about 20 minutes. Remove the foil and return the pastry to the oven for a further 5 minutes to brown. While still warm, remove the pastry shell from its pan and put it on a wire rack to cool. Place the pastry shell on a pretty plate and fill with the chilled, drained Ratatouille. Pour over the cream in a spiral, and sprinkle with the parsley.

Serve immediately or the pastry will lose its crispness.

# GARLIC CHEESECAKE TART

SERVES 6

### INGREDIENTS

225 g/8 oz shortcrust pastry

1 head garlic (about 12 cloves)

handful of parsley

handful of watercress or spinach

175 g/6 oz cream cheese

100 ml/4 fl oz single cream

3 eggs, beaten

salt and freshly ground black pepper

Preheat the oven to 425°F/220°C/gas 7. Line an 20-cm/8-inch flan dish with the pastry and cover with foil. Fill with baking beans and bake blind for 10–15 minutes until firm. Remove the baking beans and foil and leave the pastry shell to cool.

Simmer the unpeeled garlic cloves for 25 minutes until soft. Drain and, when cool, mash to a paste.

Cook the parsley and watercress or spinach in a pan of boiling water for 7–10 minutes until tender. Drain and refresh under cold water. Squeeze out the excess liquid, and chop finely. Mix with the garlic paste, seasoning with a little salt and pepper to taste. Spread the mixture over the bottom of the cooked pastry shell.

Mash the cream cheese with the cream and a little salt and pepper until smooth. Add the beaten eggs. Pour over the garlic paste and bake at 350°F/180°C/gas 4 for about 25 minutes until just set. Serve warm.

◀ *Tarte Marie-Odile*

# CRAB-STUFFED MUSHROOMS

SERVES 6 ~ 8

*These mushrooms are very rich and very delicious. Even people who usually think they do not like seafood will love this stuffing.*

### INGREDIENTS

24 large, flat mushrooms

25 g/1 oz butter

4 spring onions, chopped

1 garlic clove, crushed

½ tsp salt

½ tsp cayenne

4 Tbsp dry breadcrumbs

4 Tbsp double cream

350 g/12 oz fresh crab meat, picked over, or frozen or canned, well drained

Parmesan cheese

Clean the mushrooms and separate the stems from the caps. Meanwhile, finely chop the stems. Steam the mushrooms for 5 minutes, then set aside.

In a frying pan over medium heat, melt the butter. Add the chopped stems, spring onions, and garlic and cook for 8–10 minutes or until most of the liquid has evaporated. Add the salt, cayenne, breadcrumbs and cream, and mix well. Gently stir in the crab meat and cook until just heated through.

Stuff the mushroom caps with the crab mixture, mounding a little on each top. Sprinkle with Parmesan cheese. Arrange on a lightly greased baking sheet. Bake at 350°F/180°C/gas 4 for 10 minutes, then grill for 2–3 minutes until the cheese turns golden brown.

# SORBET TOMATOES

SERVES 4

### INGREDIENTS

2 large beefsteak tomatoes

salt

2 garlic cloves, crushed

freshly ground black pepper

generous handful of fresh mint leaves

juice of 1 large lemon

2 tsp sugar

2 egg whites

sprigs of mint, to serve

Halve the tomatoes horizontally. Scoop out and reserve the seeds and cores.

Sprinkle the insides of the tomato shells with a little salt and turn them upside down to drain. Smear the inside of each tomato shell with the crushed garlic and sprinkle with plenty of pepper.

Press the tomato seeds and cores through a sieve to extract the juice, and make up to 150 ml/¼ pint with water. Combine the mint leaves with lemon juice and sugar in a blender. The mixture should not be too smooth.

Pack into an ice-cube tray and freeze for about an hour, until crystalline but still slightly mushy.

Whip the egg whites with a couple of pinches of salt until it forms soft peaks, and fold it into the semi-frozen mint mixture. Freeze until firm, stirring occasionally.

Pile the sorbet into each tomato half and garnish with a sprig of mint.

# PAPAYA CRAB

SERVES 4

*According to Jamaican folklore, a goat tied to a papaya tree won't be there in the morning.*
*This luxurious combination of papaya and crabmeat will disappear a lot quicker.*

### INGREDIENTS

2 ripe papayas, each about 300 g/10 oz

4 Tbsp whipped cream

100 ml/4 fl oz mayonnaise

Garlic Dressing (page 180) or garlic juice to taste

lime or lemon juice

freshly ground white pepper

350 g/12 oz crabmeat

Split the papayas and remove the seeds and 'strings'. Mix the whipped cream with the mayonnaise. Homemade mayonnaise is much richer than commercial brands, so you may need to add a little more whipped cream to lighten it.

Flavour to taste with garlic dressing or garlic juice, lime or lemon juice and a little white pepper. This dressing should be delicate.

Combine the dressing with the crabmeat and pile into the papaya halves. Serve chilled.

### COOK'S TIP
For Melon Crab, use two small melons, halved and deseeded, instead of the papayas. The fragrant, orange- or peach-fleshed varieties of melon, such as Charentais and Canteloupe, are particularly good for this.

# PRAWN PANCAKES

SERVES 4 ~ 6

## INGREDIENTS

675 g/1½ lb cooked prawns in their shells

juice of ½ lemon

1 small onion, quartered

2 garlic cloves, coarsely chopped

300 ml/½ pint dry white wine

½ tsp dill

½ a bayleaf

3–4 parsley stalks

sprig of thyme

115 g/4½ oz plain flour

2 eggs, beaten

90 g/3½ oz butter

300 ml/½ pint milk

100 ml/4 fl oz cream

salt and freshly ground white pepper

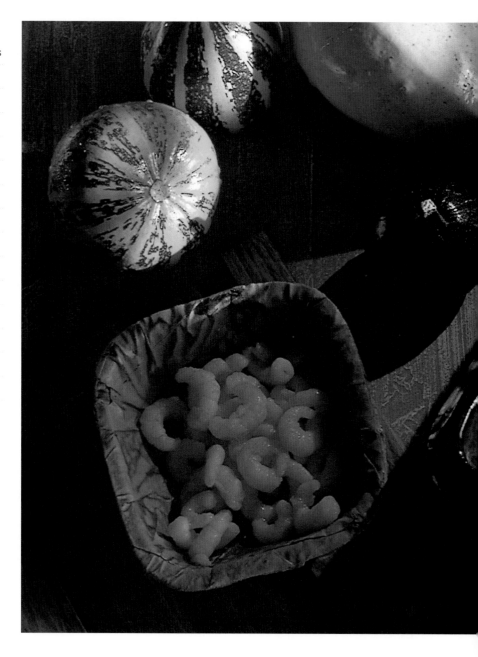

Wash and peel the prawns, cover and put it into the refrigerator. Simmer half the shells with the lemon juice, onion, garlic, wine and herbs in a large saucepan for 30 minutes.

Make the pancake batter by sifting 100 g/4 oz of the flour with a good pinch of salt. Stir in the eggs. Then melt 2 tablespoons of the butter and add to the flour together with enough milk to make a fairly thick batter. Leave the batter to stand in the refrigerator for at least 1 hour.

Strain the prawn shell stock and reduce, if necessary, to about 150 ml/¼ pint. Melt 2 tablespoons of butter and add the remaining flour. Stir over a moderate heat, without browning, for a couple of minutes. Add the stock and simmer for a further 5 minutes.

Remove from heat and add the prawns and cream. Adjust the seasoning and keep warm.

To cook the pancakes, stir the chilled batter well (you may need to add a little more milk at this stage). Fry 1 tablespoonful at a time in a buttered pan, keeping each pancake warm as it is cooked. When all the pancakes have been cooked, fill them with the prawn mixture and arrange in a buttered baking dish. Dot with the remaining butter and brown under a moderate grill for 5 minutes to heat through. Serve immediately.

# GRIDDLED AUBERGINE AND GOAT'S CHEESE SALAD

### SERVES 4

*In this marinated salad, the spiced aubergine slices are grilled and served hot with goat's cheese. Do try a true goat's cheese, it is so good. The real thing should be eaten at its freshest.*

### INGREDIENTS

I aubergine, thinly sliced

olive oil, for frying

90 g/3½ oz soft goat's cheese, sliced

#### MARINADE

1½ tsp cumin seeds

½ tsp coarse sea salt

100 ml/4 fl oz red wine

2 Tbsp olive oil

I Tbsp red wine vinegar

salt and freshly ground black pepper

I garlic clove, crushed

I Tbsp chopped fresh mint

I tsp sugar

Make the marinade. Heat a small frying pan, then add the cumin seeds and dry fry them for 30–45 seconds, until fragrant and starting to brown. Turn the seeds into a mortar with the sea salt and pound them with a pestle until finely ground. Alternatively, crush with the end of a rolling pin.

Transfer the spice mixture to a shallow dish and add the remaining marinade ingredients. Add the aubergine slices, turning to coat well, then leave for at least 30 minutes.

Shake the aubergine slices dry, and reserve the marinade. Cook the slices with a little oil in a griddle pan or frying pan. Place in an ovenproof dish and top with the sliced cheese.

Drizzle with the remaining marinade then grill under moderate heat until lightly browned. Serve with crusty bread and a juicy tomato salad.

# ROASTED PEPPERS IN OIL

SERVES 4

*Roasted peppers in olive oil are quintessential Mediterranean fare, eaten in a variety of guises throughout the Mediterranean and Middle East, but they are also the national dish of Romania, eaten with slabs of white brynza cheese (similar to feta) or with garlicky, grilled meatballs.*

### INGREDIENTS

3 each: red, yellow and green peppers (or 8–9 of any one kind)

1 Tbsp salt

100 ml/4 fl oz wine vinegar

100 ml/4 fl oz water

100 ml/4 fl oz extra-virgin olive oil

5 garlic cloves, chopped

2 tsp paprika

½ tsp sugar, or to taste

sprig of thyme, to serve

50–75 g/2–3 oz diced brynza or feta cheese, to serve

handful of black olives, to serve

Roast the peppers by placing them directly on the top of the cooker and letting them cook just slightly away from the heat, until they are lightly and evenly charred. Alternatively, place the peppers on a baking sheet and grill them for about 15 minutes on each side, turning so that they brown in spots in an even manner.

Wrap them in a clean teatowel or place them in a bowl or pan with a tight-fitting lid or in a plastic or paper bag, and seal tightly. Leave for about an hour until cool.

Remove the skin, using a paring knife. Run them under cold water carefully to get rid of excess bits of charred black skin, but not for long, as they may lose their smoky flavour too. When the peppers are peeled, use a paring knife to cut off the stem end, and remove both it and the seeds. Save any juices inside.

Cut the peppers into halves lengthwise, and combine them with their roasting juices, the salt, vinegar, water, olive oil, garlic, paprika and sugar, as desired. Leave to chill for at least 2 hours, or overnight if possible.

Serve at room temperature as an antipasto, garnished with thyme. Sprinkle over the diced cheese and arrange the black olives on the platter.

# CHEESE AND GUACAMOLE PIZZA WEDGES

MAKES 24 APPETIZER WEDGES

*Tortillas baked with cheese are popular pizzas in the Southwest of America. Mexican restaurants in Arizona serve them on giant tortillas, but unless you make your own, these are not readily available. This recipe uses 20-centimetre/8-inch tortillas, which are easy to find, and are a good size for appetizers.*

### INGREDIENTS

1 ripe avocado

1 large garlic clove, chopped

2 Tbsp bottled pickled jalapeño pepper, chopped

2 tsp juice from pickled jalapeños

½ tsp salt

6 flour tortillas

175 ml/6 fl oz bottled salsa

175 g/6 oz grated Cheddar cheese

To make the guacamole, mash the avocado with a fork. Add the chopped (or pressed) garlic and the chopped bottled jalapeño peppers, along with 2 teaspoons liquid from the bottle. Stir in the salt. Store in the refrigerator until ready to serve.

To make the pizzas, lightly toast the tortillas (easiest in a toaster oven). Remove from the oven and top each tortilla with 2 tablespoons of salsa, then a quarter of the grated Cheddar cheese. Grill for about 3 minutes, until the cheese melts.

To serve, cut each tortilla into quarters. Top each quarter with a teaspoon of guacamole.

# RIPE TOMATO AND BASIL BRUSCHETTA

SERVES 4

*This delicious, oily, garlicky treat is on the menu all over northern Italy. It is one of the best things
to eat in the summer, when you have good bread, good tomatoes and good oil.*

### INGREDIENTS

4 thick slices of Italian bread
(or French bread, if not available)

100 ml/4 fl oz olive oil
(or more, as needed)

6 very ripe, flavourful tomatoes, diced

handful of fresh, sweet basil leaves, torn

4 garlic cloves, chopped

coarse sea salt, to taste

Brush the bread with several tablespoons of the olive oil, then toast it on a baking sheet at 425°F/220°C/gas 7 for about 15 minutes, turning once or twice, or until crisp and golden brown.

Combine the tomatoes with the rest of the olive oil, basil and garlic, sprinkle with coarse sea salt, and serve on the bread.

# LEMON CHICKEN SOUP WITH HERB DUMPLINGS

SERVES 6

*This delicate soup with herb-and-garlic-scented dumplings was inspired by* avgolemono,
*the classic Greek lemon and chicken soup.*

### INGREDIENTS

100 g/4 oz soft white breadcrumbs

1 garlic clove, crushed

1 Tbsp parsley, finely chopped

1 tsp dill, finely chopped

1 tsp mixed fresh herbs

salt and freshly ground black pepper

1 egg, beaten

a little seasoned plain flour

1.1 litres/2 pints well-flavoured
chicken stock

juice of 2 large lemons

6 sprigs of fresh dill, to serve

6 slices of lemon, to serve

Make the dumplings. Mix together the breadcrumbs, garlic, parsley, dill and mixed herbs. Season with a little salt and black pepper, and add enough of the beaten egg to form a soft dough.

Shape the mixture into small balls, about the size of a large marble, and roll each in the seasoned flour.

Bring the stock to the boil in a large saucepan and poach the dumplings for 5–8 minutes.

Remove from the heat, add the lemon juice, and adjust the seasoning.

Just before serving, add a sprig of dill and a slice of lemon to each bowl.

# SNACKS &
# SAVOURIES

# FRIED GARLIC HALOUMI

MAKES ABOUT 16

### INGREDIENTS

225 g/8 oz haloumi cheese
(available from most Greek delicatessens)

3–4 garlic cloves, crushed

1 Tbsp fresh mixed herbs, bruised and
torn into small pieces

300 ml/½ pint olive oil

### COOK'S TIP
Strained, the left-over oil is marvellous for salad dressings and marinades.

Cut the cheese into 2.5-cm/1-inch cubes and pack them into a shallow soufflé dish in a single layer. Sprinkle over the crushed garlic and herbs, and pour over the olive oil to cover the cheese cubes.

Cover the dish with a plate and leave in a cool place for at least 12 hours so that the flavours of the garlic and herbs permeate the cheese.

To cook the haloumi, drain off the garlic oil and fry the cheese for about 6 minutes in a few tablespoonfuls of the oil until golden all over.

Serve immediately with cocktail sticks. To serve as a first course, cut the haloumi into thick slices, marinate, fry and serve with a sharp gooseberry sauce.

# PIPERADE

SERVES 3 ~ 4

*This makes a tasty brunch and is filling enough to keep you going until dinner time.*

### INGREDIENTS

25 g/1 oz butter

1 medium onion, thinly sliced

1–2 garlic cloves, crushed

1 red pepper, seeded and thinly sliced

2 large tomatoes, skinned, seeded
and coarsely chopped

4 eggs

salt and freshly ground black pepper

slice of hot buttered toast per
person, to serve

1 Tbsp parsley, chopped, to garnish

Melt the butter in a heavy saucepan, and cook the onion, garlic and pepper for 15 minutes. Add the tomato and cook for a further 5 minutes.

Beat the eggs together with a little salt and pepper and pour this mixture over the vegetables.

Reduce down the heat and stir the mixture until the eggs are thick and the texture is creamy. Be careful not to overcook them.

Spread the mixture on hot, buttered toast and serve, sprinkled with parsley.

### COOK'S TIP
For a more substantial version, add 225 g/8 oz of cubed, cooked ham with the tomatoes.

*Piperade* ▶

# GARLIC BUTTERED NUTS

### INGREDIENTS

225 g/8 oz shelled almonds, cashews or peanuts, or a mixture

25 g/1 oz butter

1 Tbsp oil

2–3 garlic cloves, finely crushed

rock salt

Loosen and remove the almond skins by pouring boiling water over them and refreshing in cold water. Rub the brown skins off the peanuts and discard.

Melt the butter and oil with the garlic in a heavy frying pan and toss the nuts in it over a moderate heat for 3–5 minutes or until they are crisp and golden on the outside.

Drain on kitchen paper and sprinkle with rock salt. Serve warm.

### COOK'S TIP
To make Devilled Garlic Nuts, add a little cayenne to the rock salt.

# OMELETTE WITH MOUSSERONS

SERVES 4

*This omelette from southwestern France has a real flavour of the autumn. Use any mushrooms, especially porcini, or a mixture of common cultivated brown mushrooms with a few delicious dried mushrooms.*

### INGREDIENTS

350 g/12 oz mousserons, diced

1 slice (about 50 g/2 oz) prosciutto (or other strong-flavoured raw ham), diced

3 garlic cloves, chopped

1–2 Tbsp chopped fresh parsley

2–3 Tbsp olive oil or butter

salt and freshly ground black pepper

8–10 eggs, lightly beaten

2–4 Tbsp milk

Lightly sauté the mushrooms together with the ham, garlic and parsley, in about half the olive oil or butter, until just tender. Season to taste with salt and pepper, and set aside.

Combine the eggs with the milk.

Heat a small omelette pan if you are going to make 4 individual omelettes or a large pan for a single large omelette or for 2 medium sized omelettes. For 4 individual omelettes, add 1–2 teaspoons of olive oil or butter to the hot pan, then pour in a quarter of the egg mixture. Cook for a few moments, then spoon in a quarter of the mushroom mixture. Roll the sides over and roll the omelette out of the pan. Repeat with the remaining ingredients.

To make a single large omelette, do the same, using all the egg and filling in one go. For 2 medium-size omelettes, do the same but with half the mixture in each. Serve immediately.

*Garlic Buttered Nuts* ▶

# TOMATO-CHILLI EGGS

### SERVES 4

*In the Yucatán this classic dish would come sandwiched between two crisp tortillas, but with tortillas at the bottom only, the dish is more visually appealing.*

### INGREDIENTS

400 g/14 oz fresh or
canned tomatoes, chopped

1 onion, chopped

3 garlic cloves, crushed

1–2 fresh chillies, chopped

salt and freshly ground black pepper

large dash of ground cumin

3 Tbsp olive oil

1 plantain, peeled and diced

1 Tbsp butter

4 tostadas

refried beans, seasoned with cumin

4 or 8 poached or fried eggs, kept warm

1 red pepper or 1 fresh large red
mild chilli, roasted, deseeded, stemmed
and peeled, then cut into strips

3–4 Tbsp cooked green peas, warm

3 Tbsp diced smoked ham

2 Tbsp chopped fresh coriander

75 g/3 oz flavourful white cheese
(such as feta) or mild white cheese
(such as caerphilly), diced

In a blender or food processor, purée the tomatoes with the onion, garlic, chillies, salt and pepper and cumin.

Heat the oil in a frying pan, then ladle in a little of the sauce and cook until the sauce reduces in volume and becomes almost paste-like. Ladle in some more sauce and repeat. Finally, pour in the remaining sauce, and simmer together for 5–10 minutes.

Keep warm.

Lightly brown the plantain in butter. Set aside and keep warm.

Spread the tostadas with warm refried beans, then top each with 1 or 2 poached or fried eggs.

Spoon the warm tomato sauce around or over the egg, then sprinkle with the diced plantain, roasted peppers or chillies, peas, ham, coriander and cheese.

# JAZZED CECILS

SERVES 4 ~ 6

| |
| --- |
| 450 g/1 lb minced beef |
| 1 small onion, grated |
| 50 g/2 oz fresh white breadcrumbs |
| 2–3 garlic cloves, crushed |
| 2 tsp tomato purée |
| 1 tsp sugar |
| 1 tsp paprika |
| 2 dashes of Tabasco sauce |
| 1 Tbsp mixed fresh herbs |
| 1 egg, beaten |
| salt and freshly ground black pepper |
| 50 g/2 oz seasoned plain flour |
| 4 Tbsp butter |
| 2 Tbsp oil |
| 250 ml/8 fl oz thick natural yoghurt |
| 1 Tbsp chopped chives |
| 1 Tbsp chopped parsley |

Combine the minced beef, onion, breadcrumbs, garlic, tomato purée, sugar, paprika, Tabasco sauce, herbs and egg. Season with salt and pepper.

Mould the mixture into small balls, about the size of a large marble, and roll these in the seasoned flour.

Fry the balls in the butter and oil for 5–10 minutes. Drain on absorbent kitchen paper and keep warm.

Make the dip. Mix together the yoghurt, chives and parsley and season with salt and pepper.

Serve the cecils with cocktail sticks with the yoghurt dip to one side in a separate dish.

# ROLLED OMELETTE WITH GOAT'S CHEESE FILLING

### SERVES 4

*The goat's cheese filling is tangy and fresh, and the eggs are delicate when gently cooked in the fragrant olive oil.*

### INGREDIENTS

8 eggs, lightly beaten

2–3 Tbsp milk

salt and freshly ground white pepper

4–5 Tbsp extra-virgin olive oil

½ or more green chilli, finely chopped

2 garlic cloves, finely chopped

100–175 g/4–6 oz goat's cheese

3 Tbsp chopped dill

3 Tbsp chopped fresh coriander

soured cream to taste (optional)

Prepare 4 individual omelettes, using 2 eggs for each, mixed with a little milk. Pour 1–2 tablespoons of olive oil into the omelette pan, and warm but don't overheat – it should smell fragrant and be almost smoking, but not quite.

Pour in the required amount of beaten egg, and cook for a few moments over a low heat, lifting the edges from the sides and letting the runny egg flow under. When the egg is nearly set, sprinkle in a quarter of the chilli, garlic, goat's cheese, dill and coriander, and fold over.

Roll out of the pan and serve hot, with each omelette topped with a scoop of soured cream, if wished.

# GARLIC TAPENADE

### SERVES 6

*On small pieces of toast, this snack can serve as a canapé.*

### INGREDIENTS

100 g/4 oz black olives

2–3 garlic cloves, coarsely chopped

75 g/3 oz canned anchovies

1 Tbsp capers

100 ml/4 fl oz olive oil

medium French loaf, thinly sliced

Stone and coarsely chop the olives and blend them with the garlic, anchovies and capers. Add the olive oil gradually.

Toast the bread on one side. Spread the untoasted side thickly with the mixture, and cook under a hot grill until the edges are well browned. Serve warm.

This tapenade can also be served on fingers of crisp, buttered toast.

*Rolled Omelette with Goat's Cheese Filling* ▶

# AUBERGINE AND TOMATO GALETTE

SERVES 4

*This is delicious as a supper dish, but it could easily be stretched to feed more as an appetizer. Although it takes some time to prepare, the work can all be done in advance so that the galette can be baked at the last moment.*

### INGREDIENTS

butter, for greasing

6 large eggs, beaten

4 Tbsp milk

salt and freshly ground black pepper

olive oil, for frying

1 large aubergine, sliced

4 tomatoes, sliced

1–2 garlic cloves, thinly sliced

100 g/4 oz Mozzarella, thinly sliced

### SAUCE

150 ml/¼ pint soured cream

150 ml/¼ pint thick plain yoghurt

2 Tbsp chopped chives

grated rind and juice of ½ lemon

Preheat the oven to 400°F/200°C/ gas 6, and butter a round gratin dish, the same diameter as your omelette pan. Beat the eggs with the milk and a little seasoning, then use the mixture to make 3 fairly thick omelettes. Stack the finished omelettes on absorbent kitchen paper until required. (If you wish, finish the top of each omelette under a hot grill to save turning them over in the pan.)

Heat 2–3 tablespoons of olive oil in a pan. Add the aubergine and cook until just tender and lightly browned, adding more oil as necessary. Place one omelette in the bottom of the buttered dish, then arrange half the aubergine slices in a layer on top.

Season lightly, then cover with half the sliced tomatoes and garlic. Season again and top with a third of the Mozzarella. Repeat the layers, finishing with an omelette topped with Mozzarella.

Bake in the preheated oven for 20–25 minutes, until the galette is piping hot and the Mozzarella has melted and is lightly browned.

Mix together all the ingredients for the sauce while the galette is baking. Serve the galette cut into quarters, with the sauce spooned over and around it.

# MAMMY PATTIES

MAKES 25 ~ 30

*A cocktail version of West Indian Patties.*

## INGREDIENTS

2 medium onions, finely chopped

1½ Tbsp oil

1½ tsp turmeric

1 tsp ground coriander

½ tsp ground cumin

½ tsp paprika

½ tsp garam masala

pinch of cayenne or chilli powder

3 garlic cloves, crushed

100 g/4 oz grated carrot

½ tsp sugar

350 g/12 oz minced beef

175 g/6 oz cooked rice

salt and freshly ground black pepper

350 g/12 oz puff pastry

3 Tbsp milk

Preheat the oven to 425°F/220°C/ gas 7. Cook the onions in hot oil with all the spices, except for ½ teaspoonful of turmeric, for several minutes, stirring well during cooking.

Add the garlic, carrot and sugar, and cook on a lower heat for a further 10 minutes or until the onion is transparent.

Add the beef and stir over a medium heat for about 7 minutes or until the meat has lost its pinkness.

Stir in the cooked rice and season to taste. Leave to cool.

Roll out the puff pastry thinly on a well-floured board. Stamp it into 75-cm/3-inch rounds, using a glass or a special pastry cutter.

Form the trimmings into a ball, roll out again, and repeat. Stack the rounds sifting a little flour between each, and store in the refrigerator.

To fill the patties, pile a generous teaspoonful of the meat filling slightly to one side of the centre of each pastry round. Brush all round the rim with a little water and fold over the pastry to form a semicircle. Press the wetted wedges together with a fork and prick the top.

Dissolve the remaining turmeric in a little hot water and the milk.

Space the filled patties on well-greased baking sheets, brush them with the turmeric milk, and bake until crisp and brown. Serve warm.

# OAXACA EGGS

SERVES 4

*Cooking eggs to make a flat omelette then cutting it into strips makes an intriguingly different egg dish.*

### INGREDIENTS

900 g/2 lb tomatoes

6 small to medium sized onions, peeled and halved

10 garlic cloves, whole and unpeeled

2–3 Anaheim or 1 red pepper or other mild red chillies, roasted, peeled and sliced

3 fresh green chillies (such as serranos), thinly sliced

6 Tbsp oil

salt and freshly ground black pepper

dash of cumin

dash of dried oregano

dash of sugar

8 eggs, lightly beaten

2 Tbsp chopped fresh coriander, to garnish

a little chopped fresh chilli (optional), to garnish

In an ungreased, heavy-based saucepan, lightly char the tomatoes, turning once or twice. Allow to cool.

Cut up the tomatoes and place in a blender or food processor with their skins. Lightly char the onions and garlic. Cut up the onions and add to the blender or food processor, then squeeze the garlic cloves out of their skins and add with the chillies. Whirl until a smooth purée is formed.

Heat 2 tablespoons of oil in a frying pan, then ladle in the sauce. Cook over high heat until it thickens and condenses.

Season to taste with salt and pepper, cumin, oregano and sugar to balance the acid-sweetness. Set aside.

Make flat omelettes, like thin pancakes, in the remaining oil, cooking about 2 eggs at a time and turning them over. Stack on a plate, and slice into noodle-like ribbons.

Heat the omelette strips in the sauce until warmed through, then garnish with coriander and a little fresh chilli.

# SCARBOROUGH EGGS

SERVES 2

*This is the perfect dish for a light lunch. Serve it with plenty of crusty bread*

*and a green salad.*

### INGREDIENTS

40 g/1½ oz butter

1 garlic clove, crushed

½ Tbsp chopped parsley

½ tsp chopped fresh sage

2–3 blades of fresh rosemary, bruised

½ tsp fresh thyme

salt and freshly ground black pepper

4 fresh eggs

Melt the butter over a low heat and add the garlic, herbs and seasoning. Cook gently for about 5 minutes until the garlic is transparent. Bring a small saucepan of water to the boil and cook the eggs for 3½–4 minutes. Shell them.

Add the eggs to the herb and garlic butter and turn them for a minute. Remove the rosemary blades and serve immediately.

# BAKED EGGS WITH GREEN PEAS AND CREAM

### SERVES 4

### INGREDIENTS

450 g/1 lb green peas, fresh
(shelled weight)

1 tsp sugar

sprigs of fresh mint

50 g/2 oz butter

salt and freshly ground black pepper

8 eggs

1 garlic clove, finely crushed

150 ml/¼ pint single cream

Preheat the oven to 400°F/200°C/ gas 6. Boil the peas with the sugar and mint for 10–15 minutes or until just tender.

Drain, discarding the mint, and mash to a rough purée.

Stir in the butter, and season with salt and pepper to taste.

Divide the pea purée among 4 greased ramekin dishes and break 2 eggs over the top of each.

Mix the garlic into the cream and pour over eggs. Bake for 7–10 minutes, until the eggs are just set. Serve immediately.

### COOK'S TIP

'Mushy peas' are a woefully neglected vegetable, and this is a delicious and unusual way of serving them. Warm the contents of a 425-g/15-ounce can, beat in a little butter, season with plenty of salt and pepper, and proceed as above.

# GARLIC SCONES

### MAKES 12

### INGREDIENTS

225 g/8 oz plain flour

2½ tsp baking powder

salt and freshly ground white pepper

50 g/2 oz butter or margarine

2 garlic cloves, finely crushed

150 ml/¼ pint milk and water, mixed

Preheat the oven to 450°F/230°C/ gas 8. Then sieve the dry ingredients together and rub in the butter or margarine until the mixture resembles fine breadcrumbs.

Add the crushed garlic and enough of the milk to form a soft, but not wet, dough. Divide the dough in two, dust with flour and press each half into a round about 2 cm/¾ inch thick.

Put each round on a baking pan and divide into 6 sections with a knife, but do not separate the pieces.

Bake for 10–15 minutes until the scones are brown and well risen, and the underside sounds hollow when gently tapped.

Serve warm, split and buttered.

### COOK'S TIP

Add 75 g/3 oz of coarsely chopped Cheddar cheese to the dough before adding the milk and water.

# EGGS SCRAMBLED WITH TOMATOES, CHILLIES AND TORTILLAS

SERVES 4

*Scrambled with tomatoes, chillies, garlic and spices, with a handful of crisp tortilla chips stirred in, eggs make a marvellous supper or brunch dish.*

### INGREDIENTS

8–10 corn tortillas, cut into 1-cm/½-inch strips (or several large handfuls not too salty or oily tortilla chips)

100 ml/4 fl oz vegetable oil

6 garlic cloves, chopped

1 green pepper, diced

½ jalapeño or other green chilli, thinly sliced or chopped

40 g/1½ oz butter

1½ tsp ground cumin

5 ripe tomatoes, coarsely chopped

8 eggs, lightly beaten

3 Tbsp chopped fresh coriander, to garnish

3–4 spring onions, thinly sliced, to garnish

Fry the tortilla strips in the oil until they are golden but not dark brown. Remove them from the oil and drain on absorbent kitchen towels. (If you are using tortilla chips, simply break them up into bite-sized pieces.)

Fry the garlic, green pepper and chilli in a third of the butter for just 1 minute, then add the cumin and tomatoes and cook over medium heat for 3–4 minutes until the tomatoes are no longer runny. Remove from the pan and set aside.

Over a low heat, melt the remaining butter in a pan. Pour in the beaten eggs. Cook over a low heat, stirring, until the eggs begin to set.

Add the reserved chilli-tomato mixture and tortilla strips and continue cooking, stirring once or twice, until the eggs are the consistency you wish. The tortilla strips should be pliable and chewy, neither crisp or soggy.

Serve immediately, topped with coriander and spring onions.

# INDIVIDUAL PESTO PIZZAS

### SERVES 4

*Homemade pesto is so good it's worth growing a crop of basil in your garden in order to have easy access.*
*These pizzas make great appetizers, but are also good as the main course for lunch.*

### INGREDIENTS

4 pieces of pitta bread
(15-cm/6-inch diameter)

1 small red onion, thinly sliced

1 small plum tomato, thinly sliced

100 g/4 oz feta cheese, crumbled

### PESTO SAUCE

25 g/1 oz fresh basil leaves
(soft stems and leaves only)

1 Tbsp pine nuts

1 large garlic clove, crushed

4 Tbsp olive oil

50 g/2 oz fresh Parmesan cheese

First make the pesto sauce. Put the basil, pine nuts, garlic, olive oil and Parmesan cheese in a blender or food processor and mix until thoroughly blended. Make ahead of time and refrigerate if you wish.

To make the pizza, toast the pitta bread. Then top each piece with 1 tablespoon of pesto sauce, a slice of onion, a slice of tomato, and finally, quarter of the feta cheese. Lightly grill to warm through.

# GARLIC ROULADE

SERVES 6

*The spinach filling in this roulade gives it a colourful green pattern when you cut into it.*
*Serve with a tomato salad to add to the colourful display.*

### INGREDIENTS

75 g/3 oz butter

25 g/1 oz plain flour

½ tsp English mustard

¼ tsp sugar

300 ml/½ pint hot milk

2 Tbsp Parmesan cheese

50 g/2 oz Cheddar or Gruyère cheese, grated

2 garlic cloves, crushed

salt and freshly ground black pepper, to taste

4 eggs, separated

675 g/1½ lb fresh or 350 g/¾ lb frozen spinach

2 Tbsp single cream

Preheat the oven to 425°F/220°C/ gas 7. Melt one-third of butter in a saucepan with the flour, mustard and sugar, and stir for a couple of minutes, not letting it brown. Stir in the hot milk, a little at a time, and simmer for 5 minutes.

Add the cheese, crushed garlic and salt and pepper. Remove from the heat, stir in 3 egg yolks, one at a time, and keep warm.

Boil the fresh spinach in lots of salted water for 5 minutes, until almost tender. Drain and refresh in cold water. Press out as much liquid as possible and chop finely. Turn into a pan with the remaining butter and a little seasoning, and cook gently for about 15 minutes to absorb all the butter. Check the seasoning and keep the mixture warm.

If you are using frozen spinach, cut the block into small pieces, using a freezer knife. Melt the butter, add the spinach pieces and cook very gently until thawed, turn up the heat a little, cook for a further 5 minutes, season to taste and keep warm.

Whip the egg whites with a pinch of salt until stiff. Beat a spoonful of egg white into the cheese sauce to loosen it up.

Carefully fold the cheese sauce into the remaining egg white and pour the mixture into a well-greased, foil-lined Swiss roll pan. Bake for 5–7 minutes, until just set.

Tip out immediately on to a teatowel rung out in hot water. Spread with three-quarters of the hot spinach purée, into which you have beaten the remaining egg yolk. Roll up as you would a Swiss roll – it helps if you gradually pull up one end of the teatowel as you go.

Put the roulade on a warmed dish. Stir the cream into the remaining spinach purée and pour around the roulade. Serve immediately.

# GARLIC BREAD

SERVES 4-6

### INGREDIENTS

1 French loaf

Garlic Butter (page 179), softened

1 tsp mixed fresh herbs,
chopped (optional)

Slice the bread evenly, taking care not to cut right through the bottom of the loaf.

Spread both sides of each slice with the softened Garlic Butter and sprinkle with herbs.

Wrap the loaf in foil and heat through in the oven for about 20 minutes.

### BAKED GARLIC CROUTONS

Unlike fried garlic croutons, these can be kept warm in the oven until they are needed. Spread slices of white bread, with the crusts removed, with softened Garlic Butter. Cut into small cubes and arrange, butter side up, on a greased baking tray. Bake at 375°F/190°C/gas 5 until crisp and golden.

### GARLIC BUNS

Slice the top third off white or wholemeal buns and scoop out most of the crumb. Crumble this and toss it in melted Clarified Garlic Butter with some poppy seeds or mixed herbs. Pile the buttered crumbs into the bun shells, replace the tops and warm through before serving.

### GARLIC PULLED BREAD

Use two forks to scoop out the insides of a fresh white loaf in bite-sized pieces, stretching them slightly. Put them on a baking sheet and drizzle with melted Clarified Garlic butter and bake at 375°F/190°C/gas 5 until crisped.

# POTATO STREAMERS

SERVES 4

### INGREDIENTS

2 large potatoes

2 garlic cloves, sliced

100 g/4 oz butter

1 Tbsp grated Parmesan cheese

salt and freshly ground black pepper

paprika

Preheat the oven to 425°F/220°C/gas 7. Peel the potatoes and cut them into 2-cm/¾-inch slices. Peel each slice round and round to form a long, thin ribbon.

Soak the ribbons in iced water for at least an hour. Drain them and pat dry with absorbent paper.

Heat the garlic and butter gently in a frying pan until the garlic becomes transparent. Remove the garlic.

Take the pan off the heat, dip each potato streamer into the hot garlic butter, and lay the streamers on a baking sheet. When all the streamers have been dipped, sprinkle the Parmesan over them and season with salt, pepper and a little paprika.

Bake until crisp and well-browned, which should take 7–12 minutes. Serve warm.

### COOK'S TIP

Deep fry the dried streamers, drain on kitchen paper, and sprinkle with garlic salt. Serve immediately.

◀ *Garlic Bread*

# GARLIC MILK LOAF

MAKES 1 LARGE LOAF OR 2 SMALL LOAVES

*Add a kick to this traditional country loaf by flavouring it with garlic. Serve warm or toasted,*
*spread with butter for a delicious snack.*

### INGREDIENTS 1

1 head garlic, about 12 cloves

300 ml/½ pint milk

450 g/1 lb plain flour, warmed

1 tsp salt

25 g/1 oz butter, melted

1 Tbsp fresh yeast

½ tsp sugar

1 egg, well beaten

rock salt

a little finely chopped garlic (optional)

Preheat the oven to 450°F/230°C/ gas 8. Blanch the separated, unpeeled, garlic cloves in boiling water for 5 minutes.

Drain and peel them, and simmer in the milk for 10–15 minutes, until tender. Then sift the flour with the salt into a large bowl and make a well in the centre.

Either sieve or blend the milk and garlic to make a smooth paste, and add the melted butter.

Cream the yeast with the sugar and add to the warm garlic milk with the beaten egg. Pour on to the flour.

Mix the ingredients, thoroughly and knead lightly until smooth. The dough should be soft.

Leave to rise, covered, in a warm place for about 1 hour.

Shape the dough into one large or two small loaves and place on a greased baking sheet. Cut several parallel slashes from end to end of each loaf, and leave to rise for 15 minutes.

Sprinkle each loaf with rock salt and a little chopped garlic, and bake for 20–30 minutes until well browned and hollow-sounding when tapped underneath.

### COOK'S TIP
Leave the garlic cloves whole or add 50 g/2 oz of pine nuts, browned in a little oil, to the dough before leaving it aside to rise.

# NEW ORLEANS-STYLE SANDWICH

SERVES 4 ~ 6

*Like other Mediterranean-style sandwiches, this is drenched in olive oil with a good whiff of garlic and*
*a few drops of vinegar. Sometimes you can find ready-made olive relish, but making it yourself means*
*you can add as much garlic as you wish, and as much olive oil, too.*

### INGREDIENTS

5 garlic cloves, chopped

25–35 black olives (such as Kalamata or
Italian oil-cured), stoned and sliced

25–35 green pimiento-stuffed olives, sliced

2 roasted, red peppers, peeled and cut
into strips

3–5 Tbsp chopped fresh parsley

about 150 ml/¼ pint extra-virgin olive oil
or other full-flavoured oil

1–2 Tbsp white wine vinegar

several pinches of oregano

1 baguette or other freshly baked,
white bread loaf

150–175 g/5–6 oz salami, sliced

150–175 g/5–6 oz mortadella, sliced

150–175 g/5–6 oz prosciutto or Parma
ham, sliced

150–175 g/5–6 oz Spanish chorizo
sausage, sliced

350 g/12 oz cups thinly sliced, mild cheese
(such as caerphilly or fontina)

Combine the garlic with the olives, peppers, parsley, olive oil, vinegar and oregano.

Slice open the bread, and hollow out some of the centre of the loaf to make room for the stuffing.

Drizzle the cut sides with some of the oily juices from the olive mixture, then fill the bottom with about ⅔ of the olive salad. Then layer the meats and cheeses, before topping with the rest of the olive mixture. Close up tightly, and chill until ready to eat.

# BOCADILLO FROM SANTA GERTRUDIS

SERVES 4

*Santa Gertrudis is a little village in the hills of the Mediterranean island of Ibiza.*
*Try one of these delicious sandwiches for breakfast.*

### INGREDIENTS

4 large crusty bread rolls, with soft, tender, slightly sour crumbs

4–8 garlic cloves, cut into halves

extra-virgin olive oil, to drizzle generously

2–3 ripe tomatoes, slightly squished or thinly sliced

sprinkling of oregano

8–12 slices Parma ham or prosciutto

8–12 slices of manchego or other mild, white cheese (such as Edam, Monterey Jack or Fontina)

Partially cut, partially break apart the bread rolls lengthwise and lightly toast. Rub the cut garlic on to the toasted cut side of the bread – the coarse edges are slightly sharp and will act as a shredder. If there is any garlic left at the end, just chop and sprinkle it on top.

Drizzle the cut, garlic-rubbed rolls with olive oil, then rub with the tomatoes and sprinkle with oregano. Layer with the ham and cheese, close up, and heat again, preferably in a pan with a heavy weight that will press the bread together as it heats through.

Serve immediately, with a few olives on the side.

# PASTA & GRAINS

# PENNE WITH MIXED MUSHROOM SAUCE

SERVES 4

*Sautéed mushrooms and asparagus pieces, simmered in a creamy tomato sauce, then tossed with quill-shaped penne and fresh basil, make a flavourful, rich Italian pasta.*

### INGREDIENTS

1 onion, roughly chopped

4 garlic cloves, roughly chopped

3 Tbsp olive oil or butter, plus a little extra to finish

350 g/12 oz mixed mushrooms, cut into bite-size pieces

salt and freshly ground black pepper

450 g/1 lb fresh tomatoes, finely chopped (or 1 x 400-g/14-oz can chopped tomatoes including juice)

¼–½ tsp sugar

350 ml/12 fl oz double cream

40 g/1½ oz fresh sweet basil, torn

350–450 g/12–16 oz penne

1 bunch thin asparagus, tough ends broken off, cut into bite-size lengths

4–6 Tbsp grated Parmesan cheese

In a large frying pan, cook the onion and garlic in the olive oil or butter, until softened. Add the mushrooms and cook, stirring occasionally to prevent sticking.

Season with salt and pepper, then pour in the tomatoes, and add the sugar. Bring to the boil and cook, stirring, a few minutes more.

Add the cream and about a third of the torn basil. Taste, adjust the seasoning if necessary, and remove the mixture from the heat.

Cook the pasta in a large pan of boiling, salted water until half done, then add the asparagus, and finish cooking. The pasta should be firm to the bite and the vegetables just tender. Drain well.

Toss the hot pasta and asparagus with the creamy tomato-mushroom sauce, then toss with the Parmesan cheese, the remaining basil, and a little extra olive oil or butter. Serve while hot on warmed plates.

### COOK'S TIP
Make the mushroom mix as interesting as possible by including pink oyster mushrooms, chanterelles, shiitakes, ordinary white mushrooms, porcini, and trompettes de la mort.

# GARLIC DILL PIZZA

SERVES 2 ~ 4

*The more garlic you add to this recipe, the more it tastes like garlic bread. Any topping that can be complemented by garlic goes well on this crust. It is great just topped with cheese.*

### INGREDIENTS

1 package active dry yeast

250 ml/8 fl oz warm water

1 tsp dried dill

2 garlic cloves, chopped

275 g/10 oz plain flour, sifted

2 Tbsp olive oil

½ tsp salt

100 g/4 oz grated cheese
(such as Mozzarella or Cheddar)

In a large bowl, combine the yeast, warm water, dill, garlic and 175 g/6 oz of the flour. Mix well to blend.

Add the oil, salt and remaining flour and stir until the dough sticks together. Place the dough on a lightly floured surface. Knead the dough for about 5 minutes until it is smooth and elastic. If the dough gets sticky, sprinkle it with a little flour.

Roll the dough into a ball and place it in a lightly oiled bowl. Cover the bowl with a clean towel and set in a warm place to rise for 1 hour until doubled in volume.

When the dough has risen, roll it into a ball to make one 30-cm/12-inch regular crust pizza or divide it in two balls to make two thin-crust 30-cm/12-inch pizzas. Allow the dough to rest for 20 minutes.

When ready to bake, place the dough in the centre of a lightly oiled pan. Roll outward toward the edges with the palm of your hand until the dough fills the pan evenly. Add the grated cheese, or topping of your choice and bake in a preheated oven at 450°F/230°C/gas 8 for 25–35 minutes.

# SPAGHETTI WITH AUBERGINE AND COURGETTE

SERVES 4

*A very simple recipe becomes something special with the addition of pine nuts and aubergine slices.*

### INGREDIENTS

olive oil, for frying

50 g/2 oz pine nuts

1 large aubergine, sliced

450 g/1 lb spaghetti

2 large courgettes, sliced

1–2 garlic cloves, crushed

2 Tbsp basil leaves and parsley

salt and freshly ground black pepper

freshly grated Parmesan cheese, to serve

Bring a large pan of salted water to the boil. Heat a little oil in a large frying pan, add the pine nuts and cook until golden. Remove with a slotted spoon and leave on a plate, then add the aubergine to the pan with more oil and fry until starting to soften and brown.

Add the pasta to the boiling salted water, return to the boil and simmer until it is still firm to the bite.

Add the courgette and garlic to the pan and continue frying for 8–10 minutes until all the vegetables are soft and golden.

Drain the pasta and add it to the pan with the herbs. Season to taste. Add the pine nuts and toss well. Serve immediately, with grated Parmesan.

# ARTICHOKE WITH MUSHROOM LASAGNE

### SERVES 4

*Artichockes pair very deliciously with porcini. Both are reminiscent of Mediterranean cuisine,
and both are very good when tossed with pasta.*

## INGREDIENTS

2 artichokes

few drops lemon juice

50–75 g/2–3 oz mixed dried wild
mushrooms or 350 g/12 oz fresh
mushrooms

100 ml/4 fl oz hot water, if using dried
mushrooms, or stock

1 onion, chopped

4 garlic cloves, roughly chopped

40 g/1½ oz butter, plus a little extra for
buttering the pasta

250 g/8 fl oz whipping cream

100 g/4 oz ricotta cheese
or soured cream

salt and freshly ground black pepper

few gratings of nutmeg

225 g/8 oz egg lasagne sheets

225 g/8 oz grated cheese (such as
Gruyère, Emmenthal, Parmesan, Monterey
Jack, or a combination)

Snap the outer leaves from the artichokes by bending them back crisply. When you reach the tender inner leaves, stop, and use a paring knife to trim the base of the artichoke. Slice off the sharp, prickly tops that are left, then cut each artichoke heart into quarters and carefully pare out the thistle-like centre.

Blanch the artichoke hearts for about 3 minutes in boiling water to which you have added a squeeze of lemon. Remove, rinse in cold water, and, when cool enough to handle, slice the hearts thickly.

If you are using dried mushrooms, rehydrate them. Remove them from the water, squeeze dry, and cut into bite-size pieces. Reserve the liquid from the mushrooms.

Lightly sauté the onion and garlic in the butter until it is softened, then add the mushrooms and artichoke slices. Raise the heat and sauté, until the vegetables are lightly browned in spots throughout.

Pour in the mushroom liquid or stock, bring to the boil, and then reduce over high heat. Pour in the light whipping cream and cook for a few minutes more.

Lower the heat, stir in the ricotta cheese or soured cream, a few drops of lemon juice, salt and pepper and nutmeg. Set aside the sauce while you cook the pasta.

Cook the pasta, according to the instructions on the package, until it is just tender. Drain carefully so that you do not break too much of the pasta, then lightly toss with a little butter, and arrange on a platter.

Pour the artichoke and mushroom sauce over, then blanket with the grated cheese, and toss lightly. Serve immediately.

# PASTA WITH TUNA AND TOMATO SAUCE

SERVES 4 ~ 6

*The addition of juicy chunks of tuna is characteristic of Italian cooking. Don't worry about using canned tuna as a substitute for fresh, as the canned is actually more authentic, although you could use left-over chunks of grilled tuna in its place.*

### INGREDIENTS

1 onion, chopped

5 garlic cloves, chopped

6 Tbsp extra-virgin olive oil, or as desired

1.25 kg/2½ lb diced tomatoes
(or 400-g/14-oz can, including the juices)

2 Tbsp tomato purée

salt and freshly ground black pepper

pinch of sugar

pinch of oregano and/or majoram, to taste

200-g/7-oz can tuna, drained

450 g/1 lb spaghetti

3 Tbsp capers, preferably salted rather
than brined (rinse well if brined)

10–15 black olives, stoned and quartered

3 Tbsp chopped fresh parsley

few Tbsp of toasted breadcrumbs
(optional)

In a frying pan, lightly sweat the onion and garlic in the olive oil until softened, then add the tomatoes and cook over medium heat until the tomatoes are juicy.

Add the tomato purée if needed, then season with salt, pepper, sugar and oregano or majoram to taste. Add the tuna to the sauce, and heat the mixture through.

Meanwhile, cook the pasta in a saucepan of rapidly boiling, salted water until it is firm to the bite, then drain the pasta.

Pour half the sauce into the pasta, and toss together with the capers and olives, then toss again with the rest of the sauce.

Sprinkle with the parsley and the breadcrumbs (if using), and serve this dish immediately.

# CHICKEN AND AUBERGINE RISOTTO

### SERVES 4

*A good risotto should be moist, and the rice should still have a little bite in the middle.*
*Serve the aubergine as a sauce on top of the risotto – it works very well indeed.*

### INGREDIENTS

I large aubergine

I Tbsp lemon juice

good pinch of saffron strands

1.1 1/2 pints well-flavoured chicken stock

3 Tbsp olive oil

I large onion, finely chopped

2–3 celery sticks, finely sliced

2 chicken breast fillets, finely diced

2 garlic cloves, finely sliced

350 g/12 oz arborio rice

2 Tbsp fresh flat-leaf parsley

salt and freshly ground black pepper

I Tbsp fresh tomato purée or
ketchup, optional

150 ml/¼ pint dry white wine

2–3 tomatoes, skinned, seeded
and chopped

Cook the aubergine over a barbecue, under a moderate grill, or in a hot oven until the skin is wrinkled and blistered and the flesh is tender. Turn once or twice during cooking. Cover with a damp cloth and leave for about 10 minutes to cool slightly, then peel off the skin. Plunge the flesh into a bowl of water with a tablespoon of lemon juice, to prevent discolouration, and leave until required. Soak the pinch of saffron strands in the hot stock.

Heat the olive oil in a large frying pan over a moderate heat, add the onion and celery, and cook until soft but not browned, then add the chicken. Cook over a slightly higher heat until the chicken is white all over, then add the garlic and the rice, tossing them in the pan juices.

Add about one-third of the stock to the pan, then bring to the boil, and simmer, stirring frequently, until all the stock has been absorbed. Add half the remaining stock and repeat the simmering process.

Drain the aubergine and squeeze with your hands, extracting as much liquid as possible, then chop the flesh roughly and blend it with the parsley and seasoning to a smooth paste. Add 1 tablespoon of tomato purée or ketchup for colour.

Stir the wine into the risotto, then add the remaining stock and continue cooking until it has a creamy consistency. Add the chopped tomatoes just before the risotto is ready, and season to taste with salt and black pepper.

# CHICKEN AND OLIVE RISOTTO

SERVES 4

*Full of chicken, tomatoes and olives, this rice dish is a classic
of the Sicilian table.*

### INGREDIENTS

½ onion, chopped

4 garlic cloves, chopped

3 Tbsp extra-virgin olive oil

400 g/14 oz risotto rice

400 g/14 oz diced tomatoes, fresh or
canned, with their juices

100 ml/4 fl oz dry white wine

1 litre/1¾ pints chicken stock,
or as needed

25 green olives, pimiento-stuffed, or about
15 black and 15 green olives, stoned and
cut into halves

1 chicken breast, poached and cut into
shreds or small pieces

several pinches of mixed Italian herbs, or

a combination of rosemary,
thyme and sage

freshly ground black pepper

100 g/4 oz Romano or other sharp
cheese, grated coarsely

1–2 Tbsp chopped fresh parsley

In a large frying pan, lightly sauté the onion and garlic in the olive oil until softened.

Stir in the rice and cook for a few minutes until lightly golden, then add the tomatoes and cook for a few more minutes.

Pour in the wine, and stir until the rice has absorbed the wine. Begin to add the stock, a few half-cups at a time, letting the rice absorb the liquid while you stir, and increasing the amounts while the rice cooks so that the liquid is absorbed more quickly.

When the rice is firm to the bite, stir in the olives, chicken, herbs, pepper (the olives and the Romano are both salty, so you probably won't need salt), cheese and parsley. Serve immediately.

# PASTA WITH RAW TOMATO SAUCE

SERVES 4

*This recipe is a classic Neapolitan combination of hot pasta with raw tomatoes, rich with olive oil,*
*basil, garlic and a crumbling of goat's cheese for fresh piquancy.*

### INGREDIENTS

10 very ripe, juicy tomatoes, diced

salt

few drops of balsamic vinegar

3 garlic cloves, chopped

4–6 Tbsp extra-virgin olive oil

several handfuls of fresh basil,
torn coarsely

few pinches of hot, chilli-pepper flakes

350 g/12 oz pasta of choice

100 g/4 oz goat's cheese, crumbled

In a large bowl, combine the tomatoes with several pinches of salt, the balsamic vinegar, the garlic, most of the olive oil (except for 1 tablespoon for tossing the cooked pasta) and the basil (plus the chilli flakes, if using). Leave in the refrigerator for several hours or at least for 30 minutes.

When ready to serve, cook the pasta until it is firm to the bite, then drain and toss with the goat's cheese and remaining olive oil. Add to the sauce, and serve immediately.

# SPAGHETTI WITH TOMATO AND CLAM SAUCE

SERVES 4

*Tiny clams are tossed on a sea of tomato-based spaghetti sauce, with a dusting of fine, green parsley and the heady scent of garlic. Be careful not to swallow the shells; larger clams are more convenient. If clams are not available, use mussels.*

## INGREDIENTS

1 kg/2¼ lb fresh clams in their shells, or mussels (removed from shells)

8 garlic cloves, chopped

100 ml/4 fl oz strong-flavoured, extra-virgin olive oil

several pinches of hot, chilli-pepper flakes, or ½–1 dried, red chilli, crushed

100 ml/4 fl oz dry white wine

225 ml/8 fl oz sieved tomatoes

1 Tbsp tomato purée

sea salt to taste

pinch of sugar

several large pinches of dried oregano, crumbled

450 g/1 lb spaghetti

2–3 Tbsp chopped fresh parsley

Cover the clams or mussels with cold, salted water, and leave for 30–60 minutes to clean. Remove from the water and drain.

Cook the clams or mussels with half the garlic in the olive oil for about 5 minutes, then add the hot pepper flakes and wine. Cook over a high heat until the sauce begins to evaporate.

Add the sieved tomatoes, tomato purée, the remaining garlic, salt, sugar (to taste) and oregano. Cover and cook over medium heat for about 10 minutes or until the clams have all popped open.

Cook the spaghetti until it is firm to the bite, then drain and toss with a few tablespoons of the sauce. Pour it on to a large platter or into bowls, and top with the remaining sauce and clams. Sprinkle with parsley and serve.

# RAVIOLI

SERVES 4

*As the amount of filling you put into each ravioli and the size you cut them out can vary so much, the amounts given per ½ quantity of the Garlic Pasta recipe (see page 80) are only a guide.*

### INGREDIENTS

225 g/8 oz spinach purée

2 garlic cloves, crushed

175 g/6 oz cream cheese or
low-fat soft cheese

2 Tbsp Parmesan cheese

I small egg, well beaten

salt and freshly ground black pepper

½ quantity of Garlic Pasta dough

Combine the spinach purée, garlic, cheese and beaten egg. Season with salt and pepper to taste and leave on one side.

On a floured surface, roll and stretch the pasta dough repeatedly until it is as thin as possible. Leave for 15 minutes to firm up a little.

Brush half of the dough sheet with water and put teaspoonfuls of the filling on the wetted half, spacing it 2.5–4 cm/1–1½ inches apart.

Fold over the other half of the dough and press down firmly round each little mound of filling.

Cut between the ravioli shapes with a sharp knife or pastry wheel to make squares of pasta with a mound of filling in each.

Boil the ravioli in lots of salted water for 5–7 minutes or until the pasta is just cooked and the filling heated through.

Drain and toss with a little butter and serve immediately, with extra butter and Parmesan cheese, and perhaps a little cream.

# MUSHROOM-RICOTTA AND SAUSAGE CANNELLONI

### SERVES 4

*Diced, sautéed mushrooms added to ricotta cheese make delicious cannelloni. If dried porcini are not available, use ordinary common cultivated mushrooms, diced and sautéed, instead.*

### INGREDIENTS

90 g/3½ oz dried mushrooms
(such as porcini)

225 ml/8 fl oz water

2 plump Italian sausages, roughly chopped

5–10 fresh common cultivated
mushrooms, diced

5 garlic cloves, chopped

175 g/6 oz ricotta cheese

6 Tbsp freshly grated Parmesan cheese

1 egg, lightly beaten

salt and freshly ground black pepper

several pinches of thyme and/or
rosemary, as desired

8 egg-roll wrappers or fresh pasta

1 kg/2 lb fresh ripe tomatoes, diced
(or 1 x 600-g/21-oz can chopped
tomatoes with their juice)

175 g/6 oz Mozzarella cheese, grated

several handfuls fresh basil leaves,
roughly torn

Place the dried mushrooms and the water in a saucepan and bring to the boil. Reduce the heat and simmer for about 5 minutes, then cover, and leave to plump up. When softened, remove the mushrooms from the pan and squeeze, saving the liquid. Roughly chop the mushrooms and strain the mushroom liquid.

Meanwhile, cook the sausages with the fresh mushrooms until lightly browned in spots. Remove from the heat and mix with the garlic, rehydrated mushrooms, ricotta cheese, half the grated Parmesan cheese, the egg, salt and pepper and the thyme and/or rosemary.

Preheat the oven to 375°F/190°C/gas 5. Place several tablespoons of the mixture onto one edge of each pasta square, then roll each into a cylinder. Layer the cannelloni in the bottom of a baking dish.

Pour the diced tomatoes over the top, along with the mushroom liquid, then sprinkle with the Mozzarella and remaining Parmesan cheese.

Bake in the oven for 35–40 minutes, until the pasta is cooked, the liquid has been absorbed, and the cheese has melted. Leave to stand a few moments, then serve, with the torn basil leaves scattered over.

# GRATIN OF MACARONI WITH WILD MUSHROOMS AND PEAS

SERVES 4

*Mushrooms and pasta are natural partners and make wonderful gratins. Add any sort of bright vegetable for variety and interest. Artichokes or asparagus can be used instead of the peas.*

### INGREDIENTS

50 g/2 oz small elbow macaroni

225 g/8 oz baby peas, fresh or frozen

salt

275 g/10 oz mixed fresh wild mushrooms, or a mixture of ordinary white mushrooms and rehydrated dried mushrooms, diced

3 shallots, chopped

3 garlic cloves, chopped

40 g/1½ oz butter

3 Tbsp snipped fresh chives

freshly ground black pepper

3–4 Tbsp double cream

25 g/1 oz each grated fontina (or Gruyère, mild white Cheddar, or Monterey Jack) and Parmesan cheese

Preheat the oven to 375°F/190°C/ gas 5. Cook the pasta in rapidly boiling salted water until it is about half tender, then remove from the heat, and drain. Toss with the peas. The pasta should not be cooked so that it becomes soft, and the peas should be still bright green.

In a large frying pan, cook the mushrooms, shallots and garlic in the butter until the mushrooms are lightly browned. Remove the pan from the heat, and add the chives. Toss the vegetables with the pasta and peas. Season to taste.

Layer half the pasta mixture in the base of a gratin or casserole dish, then drizzle with half the cream and half the cheese. Top with the remaining cheese, pouring the other half of the cream over the top.

Bake in the oven for 20 minutes, or until the pasta is heated through and the cheese has melted. If the pasta seems dry, add a little more cream. Serve immediately.

# GARLIC PASTA

SERVES 6

*Keep this dish simple or use the dough to make ravioli (see page 77).*

### INGREDIENTS

450 g/1 lb plain flour

2 eggs

1 Tbsp olive oil

juice of 2–3 garlic cloves

2 Tbsp well-drained spinach purée or
1 Tbsp tomato purée

1 tsp salt

tepid water to mix

50 g/2 oz butter

grated Parmesan cheese

Mix together the flour, eggs, oil, garlic juice, spinach or tomato paste, salt and add enough tepid water to make a stiff dough.

Knead on a well-floured surface for at least 10 minutes or until it is elastic.

Divide the dough in half. Roll and stretch each piece repeatedly until it is as thin as possible. Then leave for 15 minutes to firm up a little.

Sprinkle each dough sheet with a little flour, roll up loosely, and slice into thick ribbons with a sharp knife.

Boil in plenty of salted water for 3–6 minutes until just done, then drain, and serve immediately with butter and Parmesan cheese, or whatever sauce you fancy.

# NEAPOLITAN PIZZA

SERVES 4

*Garlic and anchovies combine to create a genuine
south Italian flavour.*

### INGREDIENTS

225 g/8 oz plain flour, sifted

1 Tbsp fresh yeast

½ tsp sugar

tepid water to mix

½ tsp salt

675 g/1½ lb ripe tomatoes, skinned,
seeded, and coarsely chopped

freshly ground black pepper

2 tsp finely chopped fresh basil

2–3 garlic cloves, finely chopped

12 anchovy fillets

175 g/6 oz Mozzarella cheese, thinly sliced

1½ Tbsp olive oil

Preheat the oven to 450°F/230°C/ gas 8. Put the sifted flour into a large bowl and make a well in the middle.

Mix the fresh yeast, with the sugar and 2 tablespoons of the tepid water in a cup and pour into the flour.

Add the salt and mix well, adding tepid water to make a stiff dough.

Knead on a well-floured board until it becomes light and elastic. Cover with a clean towel and leave in a warm place for 2–2½ hours until the

dough has doubled in size.

Roll the dough into a circle 5 mm/ ¼ inch thick, and put it onto a large, well-oiled baking sheet. Leave for 10 minutes.

Top with the tomatoes, plenty of pepper, garlic and basil followed by the anchovies and sliced Mozzarella cheese. Finally, sprinkle olive oil over the top of the pizza.

Bake for 25–35 minutes in the oven, until the dough is cooked and the cheese bubbles.

# MASSAIA MIA

SERVES 2 ~ 3

## INGREDIENTS

100 g/4 oz prosciutto or cooked ham, diced

1 small garlic clove, crushed

25 g/1 oz butter

225 g/8 oz fresh pink or green tagliatelle

3 Tbsp green peas, cooked

3 Tbsp single cream

salt and freshly ground black pepper

2 Tbsp grated Parmesan cheese, to serve

1 Tbsp chopped parsley, to serve

In a frying pan, gently heat the diced prosciutto or ham and garlic in the butter. Add the tagliatelle to boiling salted water and cook for 3–5 minutes or until just tender.

Drain the pasta and add the prosciutto or ham, garlic butter, peas and cream, and season with salt and pepper to taste.

Just before serving, sprinkle with Parmesan and parsley.

### COOK'S TIP

Heat the garlic in the butter and stir into the hot, drained pasta, together with some diced smoked salmon.

# RED BEANS AND RICE WITH TASSO AND ANDOUILLE

SERVES 6 ~ 8

*The use of two highly spiced meats means this is a very spicy dish. You can use ham hocks instead of the Tasso, but increase the amount of cayenne and black pepper, or the end result will be very mild. The addition of vegetables at the end adds crunch.*

### INGREDIENTS

450 g/1 lb dried kidney beans, picked over

2–4 Tbsp vegetable oil

2 large onions, chopped

5 sticks celery, chopped

3 green peppers, chopped

2 garlic cloves, chopped

225 g/8 oz Tasso, cubed

225 g/8 oz Andouille sausage, sliced

2 bay leaves

2 tsp salt

2 tsp ground cumin

1 tsp dry mustard

1 Tbsp fresh oregano, chopped

¼ tsp freshly ground black pepper

¼ tsp cayenne

6 spring onions, chopped

2 sticks celery, chopped

1 green pepper, chopped

4 Tbsp fresh parsley, chopped

approx 900 g/2 lb cooked rice, to serve

Soak the beans in plenty of water for at least 4 hours or overnight. Drain, rinse, and return to the large pot with 1.4 litres/2½ pints water. Bring to the boil, then reduce the heat and simmer, skimming the foam, whilst preparing the vegetables.

Meanwhile, heat the oil in a frying pan and fry the onion, with the first quantities of celery and green pepper, and the garlic until wilted. Unless you use a very large pan, it is easier to cook the vegetables in two batches. Add the vegetables to the beans, along with the Tasso, sausage, herbs and seasoning and continue simmering, stirring occasionally, for 1–1½ hours or until tender. Add extra water if necessary. Taste and adjust seasoning.

Just before serving, stir in the remaining spring onions, celery, green pepper and parsley and mix well. Serve over rice.

# MUSHROOMS AND BARLEY WITH NEW ORLEANS SPICES

SERVES 4

*This Cajun-style treatment for mushrooms and barley is very comforting and tasty. Serve as a side dish for barbecued meat or fish or as a vegetarian main course.*

### INGREDIENTS

225 g/8 oz barley

900 ml/1½ pints stock

50 g/2 oz dried mushrooms, any kind, broken into small pieces

2 Tbsp olive oil

1 onion, chopped

5 garlic cloves, chopped

½ each green and red peppers, chopped

2 fresh ripe tomatoes, chopped

1 small, hot dried red chilli, or to taste, crumbled into flakes

½ tsp each ground cumin, thyme, and paprika

salt and freshly ground black pepper

Place the barley in a saucepan with the stock. Bring to the boil, then reduce the heat, and simmer for about 40 minutes or until tender. If the barley gets too dry, add more liquid. If it is too soupy, add more barley early on, or cook the mixture over a higher heat for longer, letting the liquid evaporate.

During the last 20 minutes of cooking, add the dried mushrooms.

Heat the olive oil in a frying pan and lightly cook the onion until softened, then stir in the garlic, and green and red peppers, and cook for about 5 minutes or until softened. Add the tomatoes, red chilli, cumin, thyme and paprika, and cook over high heat until the tomatoes become thick and mushy.

Toss the onion mixture with the barley, season and serve.

# FISH &
# SEAFOOD

# TUNA AND AUBERGINE KEBABS

### SERVES 4

*These are perfect kebabs for the garden or beach barbecue or to grill indoors*
*when the season changes.*

## INGREDIENTS

450 g/1 lb fresh tuna steaks, about
2.5-cm/1 inch thick, cut into cubes

1 long, thin, Indian-style aubergine

### MARINADE

grated rind and juice of 1 lime

4 Tbsp olive oil

1 garlic clove, crushed

2 Tbsp chopped fresh oregano and parsley

salt and freshly ground black pepper

Place the tuna in a glass bowl, then add all the marinade ingredients. Stir well and leave for at least 1 hour, stirring once or twice.

Half cook the aubergine on the barbecue or under the grill, until the skin is just starting to wrinkle. Cut into 1-cm/ ½-inch thick slices. Thread the tuna and aubergine onto skewers, then brush with the remaining marinade.

Cook over a moderate heat for 5–6 minutes on each side, either on the barbecue or under a grill, basting with any remaining marinade. Serve with a rice salad.

# SMOKED HADDOCK LASAGNE

SERVES 6 ~ 8

*An interesting alternative to vegetarian or meat lasagne, the strong flavour of smoked*
*haddock perfectly complements this traditional Italian dish.*

### INGREDIENTS

12 garlic cloves, unpeeled

675 g/1½ lb smoked haddock fillets

300 ml/½ pint milk

pinch of saffron threads (optional)

½ bay leaf

1 medium onion, thinly sliced

50 g/2 oz butter

25 g/1 oz plain flour

1 Tbsp grated Parmesan cheese

3 hard-boiled eggs

salt and freshly ground black pepper

350 g/12 oz dry green lasagne

a little oil

350 g/12 oz ripe tomatoes, skinned and
thinly sliced

1 tsp chopped fresh basil

175 g/6 oz Mozzarella cheese, thinly sliced

Preheat the oven to 425°F/220°C/ gas 7. Plunge the unpeeled garlic cloves into boiling water and simmer for 20–25 minutes, until soft. Drain, peel and mash.

Poach the fish in the milk with the saffron (if used) and the bay leaf for about 10 minutes or until the flesh is firm and flakes easily.

Lift the fish carefully out of the milk, skin if necessary, and break into bite-sized pieces with a fork.

Sweat the onion in the butter until transparent, taking care not to let it brown. Stir in the flour and cook for several minutes more. Discard the bay leaf and any bits of fish skin, add the milk a little at a time and let the sauce simmer for 5 minutes.

Remove from the heat and stir in the Parmesan cheese, mashed garlic, fish pieces and the hard-boiled eggs cut into eighths. Season well with salt and pepper and leave, covered, in a cool place until needed.

Boil the lasagne in batches in lots of salted water with a little oil to stop the sheets from sticking together. They should take 10–20 minutes to cook until they are firm to the bite.

Lift each piece of cooked pasta out and run under cold water and lay on a damp tea towel.

When all the pieces of lasagne are cooked, use some of them to line the bottom and sides of a well-greased

small, deep roasting tin or large pie plate, and spread over them half the fish mixture.

Top with half of the tomatoes, sprinkled with half the basil. Add another layer of pasta, fish, tomatoes and basil, finishing with a layer of pasta on the top.

Spread the sliced Mozzarella over the top and bake for approximately 30 minutes until the top is crisped and well browned.

# AUBERGINE AND COD BAKE

SERVES 4

*A simple bake with the flavours of the Mediterranean. Serve this with a crisp green salad and crusty French bread to mop up the juices.*

INGREDIENTS

butter for greasing

2–3 Tbsp olive oil

1 aubergine, sliced

1 large onion, finely sliced

1 garlic clove, crushed

2 Tbsp capers

12 black olives, stoned

400 g/14 oz chopped canned tomatoes

1 Tbsp chopped mixed fresh herbs, such as parsley, oregano, marjoram

salt and freshly ground black pepper

675 g/1½ lb cod fillet, skinned

Preheat the oven to 400°F/200°C/ gas 6. Butter a 20-cm/8-inch ovenproof serving dish. Heat 2–3 tablespoons of oil in a large frying pan and fry the aubergine slices until tender but not brown. Drain on kitchen paper. Add a little more oil if necessary, then add the onion and cook until softened. Stir in the garlic, capers and olives, then add the tomatoes and herbs, and season to taste. Simmer the sauce for 5 minutes, until it is slightly thickened and the onions are cooked.

Pour the tomato sauce into the prepared dish. Divide the cod into 4 portions and add to the sauce. Cover the fish with the fried aubergine slices and dot with butter. Place the dish on a baking sheet if it seems very full and likely to bubble over, then bake in the hot oven for 20 minutes, until the aubergine slices are browned. Serve immediately.

# QUENELLES WITH PINK FENNEL SAUCE

SERVES 4 ~ 6

*This may be fiddly to prepare but the result is certainly worth the effort.*

## INGREDIENTS

675 g/1½ lb white fish fillets

2 garlic cloves, finely crushed

300 ml/½ pint water

½ tsp salt

100 g/4 oz butter

100 g/4 oz plain flour, sifted

2 eggs and 2 egg whites

2 Tbsp chilled single cream

salt and freshly ground black pepper

fish stock or water

225 g/8-oz head fennel

1 Tbsp finely chopped onion

2 Tbsp white wine

225 g//8 oz tomatoes, skinned, seeded and chopped

½ tsp sugar

350 g/12 oz green tagliatelle or fettucine

1½ tsp fennel seeds

Blend the fish to a smooth purée with the garlic and refrigerate. Bring the water, salt and half the butter to the boil. When the butter has melted, remove from the heat and tip in the sifted flour.

Beat over a moderate heat until the mixture leaves the sides of the pan and forms a mass.

Remove from the heat and beat in the eggs and the extra whites, one at a time. Turn into a large mixing bowl and add the raw fish and garlic purée. Beat in the cream, and season with salt and pepper to taste.

Form into 16 quenelles using two wetted serving spoons. Fill one spoon with the mixture and use the other to round the top.

Poach the quenelles as soon as they are all shaped, in a deep frying pan of barely simmering fish stock or water for 15–20 minutes. Lift them out, cover with a piece of greased foil, and keep warm.

To make the sauce, chop the fennel finely, and sweat it with the onion, wine, and half the remaining butter until tender.

Mix in the chopped tomatoes and sugar, and blend to a smooth purée.

Season with salt and pepper to taste and keep warm.

Cook the pasta in lightly salted boiling water until it still has bite, drain, toss in the remaining butter and the fennel seeds, and put in a heated serving dish.

Arrange the warm quenelles on the pasta, pour over the sauce, and serve.

### COOK'S TIP

The quenelle mixture can also be served as individual fish mousses. Pack into well-buttered individual soufflé dishes or ramekins, set them in a roasting pan, half-full of boiling water. Bake at 350°F/180°C/gas 4 until the mousses have risen and drawn away from the sides of their dishes.

# STUFFED MUSSELS

SERVES 4

*The best mussels for stuffing are the large, green-lipped variety.*

### INGREDIENTS

20 large green-lipped mussels,
on the half shell

4 Tbsp olive oil

1 large onion, finely chopped

1 red chilli, deseeded and very
finely chopped

1 small aubergine, very finely chopped

2 garlic cloves, crushed

salt and freshly ground black pepper

40 g/1½ oz fresh wholemeal breadcrumbs

flat-leaf parsley sprigs, to garnish

Preheat the oven to 425°F/220°C/ gas 7. Loosen the mussels on the half shells and arrange them on a baking sheet.

Heat the oil in a large frying pan. Add the onion and chilli and cook until starting to soften, then add the aubergine and garlic. Continue cooking for 5–6 minutes, until all the vegetables are soft and lightly browned. Season well, then add the breadcrumbs and mix thoroughly.

Pile a teaspoonful of filling into each shell over the mussel, then bake for 12–15 minutes, until piping hot. Serve immediately, garnished with sprigs of flat-leaf parsley.

# TANDOORI SOLE

SERVES 4

*You can use any firm white fish for this dish.*

### INGREDIENTS

2 tsp cumin

½ tsp turmeric

½ tsp cloves

½ tsp cardamom seeds

½ tsp chilli powder

½ tsp freshly ground black pepper

½ tsp yellow mustard seeds

1 medium onion, chopped

2 garlic cloves, finely chopped

225 ml/8 fl oz natural yoghurt

6 fillets of sole, skinned

Preheat the oven to 350°F/180°C/ gas 4. Grind the spices together and blend them with the onion and garlic. Mix the spice mixture into the yoghurt.

Place the fish in a shallow dish and pour over the spice and yoghurt mixture. Leave to marinate for about 6 hours.

Remove the fish from the marinade, wrap it in kitchen foil and bake for 30 minutes.

### COOK'S TIP

This recipe can be used for chicken. Double the amount of yoghurt, leave to marinate for 12 hours, and cook for 1 hour.

# STEAMED LANGOUSTINES

SERVES 4

*Cooked over open coals or steamed gently, langoustines are luscious when served with nothing more than lemon juice, garlic and lots of olive oil.*

### INGREDIENTS

675 g/1½ lb fresh langoustine (Dublin Bay Prawns) or jumbo prawns in their shells

100 ml/4 fl oz extra-virgin olive oil

juice of 2 lemons

1 garlic clove, crushed

salt to taste

1 bunch flat-leaf parsley, chopped

Place the langoustines or prawns in a steamer, and cook them until they have turned red, which will take about 10 minutes for langoustine, 5 minutes for prawns.

Whisk together the olive oil and lemon juice, then whisk in the salt, garlic and chopped parsley.

Serve the sauce on the side, or a little spooned over the warm seafood, and the rest in a bowl on the side for dipping. Serve immediately, along with a bowl for the discarded shells.

# LIME-MARINATED SWORDFISH WITH AUBERGINE RIBBONS

SERVES 4

*Swordfish readily absorbs the flavours of marinades. Use lime for a really fresh tang.*
*Ribbons of fried aubergine provide a striking contrast to the fish.*

### INGREDIENTS

4 swordfish steaks, about 1 cm/½ inch
thick and each weighing about 125 g/5 oz

3 Tbsp olive oil

1 small long aubergine, halved and sliced
into fine ribbons

### MARINADE

grated rind and juice of 2 limes

3 Tbsp fruity olive oil

3 spring onions, finely chopped

salt and freshly ground black pepper

1 garlic clove, crushed

1 Tbsp fresh parsley, chopped

Mix all the ingredients for the marinade in a shallow dish, then add the swordfish. Leave to marinate for 1 to 4 hours, turning the steaks in the mixture once or twice.

Heat the oil in a large frying pan. Drain the swordfish, reserving the marinade, then fry it quickly in the hot oil, allowing 2 to 3 minutes on each side. Remove the fish from the frying pan and keep it warm.

Add the marinade to the frying pan and heat it gently, then add the aubergine ribbons and cook quickly until they are soft and beginning to brown. Arrange the ribbons on the swordfish steaks before serving, spooning any remaining juices over the fish.

# RED MULLET WITH GARLIC

SERVES 6

*Tiny red mullet are best used this recipe, but if they are not available,*
*use a large one and cut it up at the table.*

### INGREDIENTS

6 Tbsp very finely chopped freshly parsley

6 garlic cloves, crushed

salt and freshly ground black pepper

6 small red mullet, cleaned

flour for coating

olive oil for shallow frying

chopped fresh parsley, to garnish

lemon wedges, to serve

In a bowl, combine the parsley with the garlic, and season with salt and freshly ground black pepper.

Place about 1 teaspoon of the garlic mixture into the cavity of each fish and rub any remaining mixture evenly over the skins. Coat the entire surface of the fish lightly and evenly with flour.

Heat the oil in a deep frying pan and cook the fish, no more than 2 at a time, for 5–7 minutes, or until crisp on the outside and cooked through. Using a slotted spoon, transfer the fish to a dish lined with absorbent kitchen paper to drain. Sprinkle with parsley and serve with lemon wedges.

# PRAWN BAKE

SERVES 6 ~ 8

*This dish is far better without the addition of extra salt during cooking, as this tends to toughen*
*the delicate texture of the prawns. If you find that the salt from the feta cheese is not sufficient*
*for your taste, then only add more at the table.*

### INGREDIENTS

3 Tbsp olive oil

2 large onions, grated

2 garlic cloves, crushed

3 Tbsp chopped fresh parsley

1 Tbsp chopped fresh dill

pinch of dry mustard

pinch of sugar

400-g/14-oz can chopped tomatoes

1 Tbsp tomato purée

450 g/1 lb fresh prawns, shelled and deveined

225 g/8 oz feta cheese, crumbled

chopped fresh dill, to garnish

Preheat the oven to 425°F/220°C/ gas 7. Heat the olive oil in a large saucepan and sauté the onions for about 5 minutes, or until softened and beginning to brown. Add the garlic, chopped fresh herbs, dry mustard, sugar, chopped tomatoes and tomato purée to the saucepan.

Simmer the mixture, uncovered, for about 30 minutes, or until the sauce has reduced and thickened slightly.

Add the prawns to the sauce in the saucepan and stir. Continue to cook for a further 3–5 minutes, or until all the prawns have turned pink and are cooked through.

Pour the mixture into an ovenproof serving dish and scatter over the crumbled feta cheese. Bake for 5–10 minutes, or until the cheese has melted. Serve immediately, sprinkled with chopped fresh dill.

# HONEY GARLIC PRAWNS

SERVES 4

### INGREDIENTS

675 g/1½ lb large, raw prawns

3 garlic cloves, crushed

juice of 2 lemons

2 tsp sugar

1 Tbsp soya sauce

2 Tbsp olive oil

freshly ground black pepper

100 g/4 oz plain flour

2 pinches salt

1 egg

150 ml/¼ pint milk and water, mixed

2 Tbsp honey

2.5-cm/1-inch root ginger, grated

2 tsp cornflour

1 Tbsp sesame seeds

Peel the prawns and cut deeply along the back of each with a sharp knife, removing the main vein. Place them in a shallow dish.

Combine the crushed garlic, lemon juice, sugar, soya sauce, half the oil and a good shake of black pepper. Pour the mixture over the prawns and leave to marinate in the refrigerator or in a cool place for 2–4 hours.

Make the batter by sieving together the flour and salt. Add the egg, the remaining oil, and finally the milk and water mixture, a little at a time, until the batter will coat the back of a spoon. Store in the refrigerator.

Drain the prawns and reserve the marinade. Dip each prawn in the batter and deep fry for 1½ minutes in very hot fat until crisp and golden.

Drain the prawns on absorbent kitchen paper and keep warm in a serving dish.

Heat the remaining marinade with the honey, ginger and cornflour. Stir constantly until the sauce thickens. Allow to simmer, still stirring, for several minutes.

Pour the sauce over the prawns and turn them gently in it until well coated. Sprinkle with the sesame seeds and serve immediately.

# GARLIC GRAVAD LAX

SERVES 6 ~ 8

*This cut salmon is ideal for a buffet lunch or dinner as it can be prepared in advance and makes an attractive addition to the table.*

### INGREDIENTS

900 g/2 lb middle-cut salmon

4 garlic cloves, crushed

100 g/4 oz salt

75 g/3 oz sugar

handful of fresh dill, chopped

Split the salmon into two halves, remove the bone, but leave the skin on.

Mix together all the remaining ingredients in a large bowl.

Place one half of the salmon, skin side down, on a large, flat serving dish and cover with half the mixture. Put the other half of the salmon over it

and top with the remaining mixture.

Weight down the salmon with a plate and leave in a cool place or refrigerator for at least 24 hours. Scrape off the mixture and serve the salmon cut into thin slices.

Serve with a soured cream, mustard and horseradish dressing with a little fresh dill added.

# MIDDLE EASTERN-STYLE GRILLED SWORDFISH

SERVES 4

*Eaten throughout the Mediterranean, swordfish is usually marinated with bay leaves, lemon and lots of olive oil, then skewered and cooked over a wood fire.*

## INGREDIENTS

1.25 kg/2½ lb swordfish

1 onion, grated

8 garlic cloves, chopped

juice of 2 lemons

100 ml/4 fl oz extra-virgin olive oil

several bay leaves

salt and freshly ground black pepper

### TAHINI SAUCE

175 g/6 oz sesame paste (tahini)

2 garlic cloves, chopped

few dashes of hot-pepper sauce

few pinches of cumin

salt and pepper

juice of 1 lemon

2 Tbsp extra-virgin olive oil

100 ml/4 fl oz water, or enough to make the consistency of a smooth, thick sauce

few sprigs fresh oregano

lemon wedges, to garnish

In a large bowl, combine the fish, onion, garlic, lemon juice, olive oil, bay leaves, salt and pepper. Marinate for at least 1 hour, preferably overnight, in the refrigerator.

Cut the fish into cubes and skewer it with the bay leaves on either soaked bamboo (30 minutes in cold water) or on metal skewers, alternating the fish cubes with the bay leaves. Though you don't eat the bay leaves, they perfume the fish delightfully.

Cook the fish over a medium-low charcoal fire for about 8 minutes, turning once or twice to cook evenly.

Meanwhile, make the sauce. Mix the tahini with the garlic, hot-pepper sauce, cumin, salt, pepper, lemon juice and olive oil, then slowly stir in the water until it has the desired consistency. Taste for seasoning.

Serve the grilled fish kebabs with fresh oregano, accompanied by lemon wedges and the tahini sauce to the side of the skewers.

# STIR-FRIED SEAFOOD WITH MINT, GARLIC AND CHILLIES

SERVES 4

*Although it takes some time to prepare the ingredients, it only takes a few minutes to cook this dish, so don't be put off by the list and enjoy!*

### INGREDIENTS

100 g/4 oz fish fillets

6 mussels

1 small uncooked crab, cleaned and chopped

100 g/4 oz squid pieces

100 g/4 oz uncooked prawns

100 g/4 oz scallops

2 garlic cloves, chopped

2 large fresh chilli peppers, chopped

1 Tbsp chopped coriander roots

1 Tbsp vegetable oil

2 Tbsp oyster sauce

2 Tbsp Nuoc Mam sauce, or light soya sauce and 1 tsp anchovy sauce, mixed well

1 red pepper, cut in strips

1 onion, thinly sliced

2 shallots, thinly sliced

4 Tbsp chopped fresh mint

Wash and prepare the seafood. Cut the fish fillets into bite-sized pieces. Scrub the mussels and remove the beards. Take the limbs off the crab and crack the shell with a hammer so the meat is easy to remove at the table. Remove the outer shell, clean out the crab body, and break into bite-size pieces. Set aside.

Put the garlic, chillies and coriander root in a blender and make a coarse paste. Put to one side.

Heat the oil and fry the garlic, chilli and coriander over medium heat. Add the seafood and stir-fry gently so the fish fillet does not break up. Add the oyster sauce and Nuoc Mam sauce. Taste, cover and simmer the mixture for a few minutes.

Remove the lid and add the red pepper, onion, shallots and mint, and stir-fry gently (the fish fillets are now even more delicate) for a couple of minutes, then remove the fish mixture from the heat.

Arrange on a large, shallow serving dish and garnish with mint or whatever herbs you happen to have around. Serve with a large bowl of steaming rice.

# MOROCCAN WHOLE FISH BAKED WITH CUMIN

### SERVES 4

*The spicy mixture of cumin, coriander and garlic, all bound up in olive oil, makes a delicious flavouring for fish. It is used here on a whole fish for roasting, but you could also use it on pieces of fish wrapped in baking parchment, then roasted in their own steam and juices, or as a paste for portions of fish to be steamed.*

## INGREDIENTS

1 whole fish, such as a striped bass or snapper, about 1.5 kg/3 lb, cleaned but with head and tail left on

1 Tbsp coarse salt

1 lemon, cut into halves (one for juice, and one to cut in wedges for a garnish)

100 ml/4 fl oz extra-virgin olive oil

3 Tbsp ground cumin

2 Tbsp paprika

4 Tbsp chopped fresh coriander

5 garlic cloves, chopped

freshly ground black pepper

Preheat the oven to 400°F/200°C/ gas 6. Wash the fish, then cut slashes on its outside skin. Rub half the salt and lemon juice into the cuts and inside the fish. Leave to sit for 15–25 minutes. Rinse with cold water, and dry with kitchen paper.

Combine the olive oil, cumin, paprika, coriander, garlic, pepper and remaining salt, and mix into a paste. Rub the paste over the skin of the fish, inside and out, also inside the slashes.

Place the fish on a baking sheet and roast for 30–40 minutes, or until the fish is done; its flesh will feel firm but not hard. Take care not to overcook.

Serve hot, accompanied by wedges of lemon, and a cruet of olive oil if desired, for drizzling.

# SALT COD FRITTERS WITH GARLIC

### SERVES 6 ~ 8

*Salt cod is generally available from delicatessens. Remember to start this recipe a day in advance because the salt cod needs soaking for 24 hours.*

### INGREDIENTS

675 g/1½ lb salt cod, soaked in cold water for 24 hours, with frequent changes of water

75 g/3 oz plain flour

salt and freshly ground black pepper

1 Tbsp olive oil

150 ml/¼ pint warm water

1 egg white

olive oil for deep frying

lemon wedges, to serve

### SKORDALIA

4 slices white bread, crusts removed

6 garlic cloves, crushed

salt

50 g/2 oz blanched almonds, ground

150 ml/¼ pint olive oil

freshly squeezed juice of 1 lemon

Make the *skordalia*. Place the bread in a food processor or blender and blend into fine crumbs. Sprinkle in 4 tablespoons of cold water and leave to soak for about 5 minutes. Add the garlic, salt and ground almonds, and process until smooth and well combined.

With the motor still running, gradually add the olive oil in a continuous stream, until the mixture is thick and smooth. Gradually add the lemon juice in the same way. Turn into a serving bowl, cover, and set aside.

Strip the skin and bones away from the salt cod and discard. Cut the flesh into 5-cm/2-inch chunks.

Make the batter for the fish. Sift the flour into a large mixing bowl with the salt and freshly ground black pepper. Drizzle the olive oil over the flour and beat in the warm water to make a smooth mixture. Allow to stand at room temperature for about 1 hour.

Beat the egg white in a clean, dry bowl until it holds stiff peaks, then fold into the batter. Heat the oil. Dip the chunks of fish into the batter, then gently place in the hot oil. Cook the fish in batches for 5–7 minutes or until crisp and golden.

Using a slotted spoon, transfer the cooked fritters to a dish lined with absorbent kitchen paper to drain. Serve the battered fritters with lemon wedges and the *skordalia*.

# FISH AND VEGETABLE CASSEROLE

SERVES 8 ~ 10

*Cod, haddock or monkfish would all be suitable types of fish to use for this dish, which originates from the Greek island of Corfu. The crucial ingredient is the garlic, and plenty of it.*

### INGREDIENTS

6 Tbsp olive oil

I large onion, sliced

900 g/2 lb small new potatoes, washed and cut into I-cm/½-inch slices

2 carrots, cut into 2.5-cm/I-inch chunks

I celery stick, chopped

salt and freshly ground black pepper

6 garlic cloves, crushed

1.25 kg/2½ lb firm white fish fillets, skinned and cut into 5-cm/2-inch chunks

4 Tbsp freshly squeezed lemon juice

Heat 4 Tbsp of the olive oil in a large, heavy saucepan and cook the onion for about 3 minutes or until softened and slightly brown.

Add the potatoes, carrots and celery, and season with salt and freshly ground black pepper. Continue to cook for a further 4–5 minutes or until the vegetables begin to soften.

Stir in the garlic and pour over enough boiling water to just cover the vegetables. Bring to the boil, cover and simmer for 10–15 minutes or until the vegetables are almost tender.

Gently stir the fish into the casserole, cover and simmer for 10–15 minutes or until the fish flakes easily. Add a little extra water if necessary. Just before the end of the cooking time, remove the cover and stir in the lemon juice and remaining olive oil. Adjust the seasoning if necessary and serve.

# MEAT &
# POULTRY

# BEEF AND AUBERGINE BIRIANI

SERVES 6

*A wonderful spicy dish for lazy entertaining. Most of it can be prepared in advance and heated through at the last moment. For special occasions, decorate with gold or silver leaf just before serving.*

## INGREDIENTS

6 Tbsp ghee or sunflower oil

450 g/1 lb shin of beef, cut into 2.5-cm/
1-inch pieces, or 450 g/1 lb cooked
diced beef

2 bay leaves

400 g/14 oz Basmati rice, rinsed

2 large onions, finely sliced

1 tsp curry paste

50 g/2 oz sultanas

75 g/3 oz creamed coconut, finely
chopped

### CURRY SAUCE

2 onions, roughly chopped

3 garlic cloves, roughly chopped

1 green chilli, seeded and chopped

1 Tbsp mild curry paste

2 Tbsp tomato purée

1 Tbsp light brown sugar

6 Tbsp ghee or sunflower oil

1 large aubergine, cut into
1-cm/½-inch dice

300 ml/½ pint cream

salt, to taste

2–3 Tbsp chopped fresh coriander

### GARNISHES

2 hard-boiled eggs, quartered

50 g/2 oz whole blanched almonds,
fried until golden brown

2–3 tomatoes, sliced

Preheat the oven to 325°F/170°C/gas 3. Heat 3 tablespoons of the ghee or oil in a flameproof casserole, brown the beef, then add enough water to cover it over. Add the bay leaves, then bring just to the boil. Cover the casserole and cook in the oven for about 2 hours.

Rinse the rice, then bring to the boil in a large pan of cold water. Stir, then cover and cook for 10 minutes. Drain and rinse thoroughly, then drain again.

Prepare the curry sauce. Blend the onions, garlic and chilli with the curry paste, tomato purée and sugar in a blender or food processor. Heat the ghee or oil in a large frying pan, add the aubergine and cook until starting to brown, then add the curry sauce and continue to fry gently for 4–5 minutes. Stir in the cream and bring almost to a gentle simmer, then add salt to taste. Remove from the heat, and set aside, ready to reheat at the last moment.

Heat the remaining ghee or oil in a large frying pan or wok, add the onions and cook until golden. Remove half with a slotted spoon, to use as garnish. Add the curry paste to the onions and cook for a further minute, then add 3 tablespoons of juices from the meat, or water, and cook the mixture for 1 minute longer.

Drain the meat and add it to the pan, or add the left-over cooked meat if using. Stir-fry until it is well heated through and has absorbed the juices. Once hot, add the cooked rice to the pan with the sultanas and chopped coconut and stir gently until piping hot. Reheat the sauce gently and add the coriander.

Serve the biriani with the prepared garnishes and with the curry sauce spooned over.

# CHICKEN WITH TOMATOES

SERVES 4

*You will need lots of saucepans to make this Brazilian dish, but it's well worth the washing-up at the end!*

## INGREDIENTS

900 g/2 lb roasting chicken, quartered

salt and freshly ground black pepper

3 Tbsp olive oil

4 onions, grated

5 garlic cloves, crushed

2 x 400-g/14-oz cans plum tomatoes, chopped finely

3 Tbsp chopped fresh parsley

1 Tbsp butter

2 Tbsp plain flour

250 ml/8 fl oz milk

4 Tbsp grated Parmesan cheese

6 egg whites, beaten to a stiff peak

Put the chicken pieces in a large saucepan, add salt and pepper, and water to cover. Bring to the boil and cook over medium heat for 20 minutes.

Meanwhile, in another saucepan, heat the oil, and fry the onions and garlic for 5 minutes. Add the tomatoes, salt and pepper and parsley, and cook uncovered for 5 minutes, so that the liquid evaporates.

In a third saucepan, melt the butter, add the flour, and stir well to combine. Add the milk and keep on stirring until the sauce thickens. Turn off the heat and reserve.

When the chicken is cooked, drain, and reserve 1 cup of liquid, skimmed of fat. Discard the rest. Leave the chicken until it is cool enough to handle, then remove the meat from the bones.

Preheat the oven to 375°F/190°C/ gas 5. Shred the chicken meat finely and add to the tomato sauce. Then add the white sauce, and check the seasoning.

Transfer the mixture to an ovenproof dish. Scatter the Parmesan cheese over the top. Using a wooden spoon, put peaks of beaten egg whites over it. Bake for 5–10 minutes, or until the whites are cooked and slightly brown. Serve with white rice and deep fried bananas.

# VENISON SAUSAGE AND AUBERGINE CASSEROLE

SERVES 4

*Venison sausages have been used for this casserole, but you can use herby or spicy sausages, whichever your prefer.*

## INGREDIENTS

2 Tbsp olive oil

8 thick venison sausages

2 slices smoked bacon, diced

1 large onion, finely chopped

1 carrot, diced

1–2 garlic cloves, sliced

150 ml/¼ pint red wine

1 large aubergine, cut into chunks

400-g/14-oz can chopped tomatoes

100 g/4 oz green lentils

1 Tbsp tomato purée

300 ml/½ pint beef stock

salt and freshly ground black pepper

parsley sprigs, to garnish

Preheat the oven to 350°F/180°C/gas 4. Heat the oil in a flameproof casserole, then add the sausages and cook them briefly until browned. Add the bacon, onion, carrot and garlic, then cover the casserole and cook slowly for 4–5 minutes.

Add the red wine, then cook rapidly until it is well reduced. Add all the remaining ingredients, then bring to the boil. Cover and cook in the preheated oven for 1 hour.

Season to taste, then garnish with parsley just before serving.

# LAMB COOKED IN FOIL

### SERVES 8

*Authentic Greek* kleftiko *is cooked to the point where the meat just falls off the bone. The secret is long, slow cooking in a foil package to allow the flavours to stay trapped inside until the meat is tender.*

### INGREDIENTS

8 lamb chops

4 garlic cloves, cut into slivers

50 g/2 oz butter, melted

3 Tbsp freshly squeezed lemon juice

salt and freshly ground black pepper

1 Tbsp dried oregano

1 Tbsp dried mint

Preheat the oven to 350°F/180°C/ gas 4. Using a small, sharp knife, make incisions in the chops and insert the slivers of garlic into them. Place each chop in the centre of a 30-cm/12-inch square piece of foil.

Distribute the remaining ingredients among the 4 chops and gather up the foil, pinching it together at the top to completely encase and seal in the chops and flavourings.

Arrange the foil packages on a baking sheet and cook for 1½–2 hours, or until the meat is cooked through and very tender. Serve the packages closed, to be opened by each diner.

# RABBIT CASSEROLED IN RED WINE

SERVES 6

*Rabbit meat is very flavourful but has no fat, so it is ideal in healthy diets.*

### INGREDIENTS

50 g/2 oz butter or lard

1 rabbit, weighing about 1.7 kg/4 lb

40 g/1½ oz plain flour

2 garlic cloves, crushed

1 large onion, finely chopped

450 ml/¾ pint red wine

5 slices lean bacon

20 small onions

450 g/1 lb potatoes

salt and freshly ground black pepper

Preheat the oven to 325°F/170°C/ gas 3. Melt half the butter, cut up the rabbit and brown it in the butter for about 5 minutes. Sprinkle the browning pieces with the flour, the crushed garlic and the finely chopped onion. Add the red wine and enough water to cover the meat. Braise the rabbit, covered, in a warm oven.

While the rabbit is cooking, dice the bacon and peel the small onions. Brown them both in the remaining butter. Set aside.

After 20 minutes, add the bacon and onions to the rabbit. Re-cover.

As the rabbit, bacon and onions are cooking, peel the new potatoes. After a further 20 minutes, add these to the rabbit.

Cook the casserole for another hour or so, season and serve.

> ### COOK'S TIP
> If you cannot find new or baby potatoes, use nicely shaped old ones, carving them a little if you have to.

*Rabbit Casseroled in Red Wine* ▶

# COTTABULLA

SERVES 8

*The origins of this old family recipe are obscured in a West Indian mist, but there is nothing vague about Cottabulla itself—a tasty cross between a cold meatloaf and a* pâté campagne.

### INGREDIENTS

225 g/8 oz stale white bread, crusts removed

900 g/2 lb minced beef

2 medium onions, finely chopped

2 eggs

1 tsp ground coriander

1 tsp dried oregano

1 Tbsp paprika

3 garlic cloves, crushed

pinch of cayenne

1 tsp sugar

salt and freshly ground black pepper

Preheat the oven to 375°F/190°C/ gas 5. Soak the bread in water, squeeze out, and crumble. Mix all the ingredients together, seasoning with plenty of salt and pepper.

Pack into a large soufflé dish, leaving a slight hollow in the middle. Cover with foil and bake for 40–50 minutes until cooked through, but still slightly pink in the middle.

While it is still hot, put a plate, slightly smaller than the baking dish, on top of the foil and weight it with some heavy cans. Leave until cold and firm, remove the weights and refrigerate until needed.

Slice into wedges and serve.

> ### COOK'S TIP
> This can also be served hot, and there is no need to weight it. Shape into patties, rolled in seasoned flour, to make sensational hamburgers.

# MEATBALLS WITH AUBERGINE AND TOMATO SAUCE

SERVES 4

*Meatballs make a welcome change to the more usual minced beef sauce for pasta.*
*Simmer the meatballs gently so that they do not break up during cooking.*

## INGREDIENTS

450 g/1 lb minced lamb

6 spring onions, finely chopped

65 g/2½ oz fresh wholemeal
breadcrumbs

1 Tbsp tomato purée

½ tsp ground turmeric

salt and freshly ground black pepper

1 large egg, beaten

freshly grated Parmesan cheese, to serve

### SAUCE

3 Tbsp olive oil

1 aubergine, cut into chunks

1 onion, finely diced

1 garlic clove, finely sliced

½ tsp ground turmeric

1 tsp ground cumin

2 x 400-g/14-oz cans canned chopped
tomatoes

1 bay leaf

salt and freshly ground black pepper

8–10 fresh basil leaves, torn

Mix all the ingredients for the meatballs together. Shape the mixture with wet hands into walnut-sized balls.

Make the sauce. Heat the oil in a large frying pan, then add the aubergine and fry gently until lightly golden. Add the meatballs, together with the onion, garlic, turmeric and cumin, and cook until the meatballs are browned all over. Add extra oil only if the meatballs are sticking.

Add the tomatoes and bay leaf with salt and pepper and bring to the boil. Simmer gently for 20 minutes, then season to taste. Add the basil leaves just before serving.

Serve with pasta, sprinkling a little Parmesan over the meatballs if wished.

# BEEF COBBLER

SERVES 6 ~ 8

### INGREDIENTS

900 g/2 lb stewing steak

50 g/2 oz seasoned flour

4 Tbsp oil

3 medium onions, cut into large chunks

4–5 garlic cloves, crushed

4–5 large carrots, cut into thick slices

2 tsp dried mixed herbs

1 tsp sugar

1 Tbsp paprika

1 Tbsp tomato purée

300 ml/½ pint red wine

300 ml/½ pint stock or water

### SCONE TOPPING

salt and freshly ground black pepper

225 g/8 oz plain flour

2½ tsp baking powder

50 g/2 oz butter or margarine

150 ml/¼ pint cold milk and water

Preheat the oven to 400°F/200°C/ gas 6. Trim the fat and membrane from the meat and cut the steak into 3-cm/1¼-inch chunks. Roll the meat in the seasoned flour and fry rapidly in the oil in batches until browned all over. Drain the meat and transfer to a large casserole and sprinkle with any remaining seasoned flour.

Fry the onions and garlic in the remaining oil until they begin to brown and add to the casserole, together with the carrots, herbs, sugar, paprika, tomato purée, wine, stock or water and plenty of salt and pepper.

Stir gently and cook the uncovered casserole for 20 minutes. Stirring once.

Cover the casserole with foil, put its lid on and cook at 325°F/170°C/gas 3 for a further 2 hours, stirring from time to time. Add more stock or water if the mixture looks dry.

To make the scone topping, sieve together the flour and baking powder and then rub in the butter or margarine until the mixture resembles fine breadcrumbs.

Add plenty of salt and pepper to season and enough milk and water to make a soft dough.

Roll out the dough to 1 cm/½ inch thick on a well-floured surface and stamp out circles 5 cm/2 inches across.

Taste the stew and adjust the seasoning, adding a little more stock or water if necessary.

Arrange the scone circles on top of the hot stew and cook, uncovered, at 400°F/200°C/gas 6 for 20–30 minutes, until the scones are puffy and well browned.

# PORK AND RED CHILLI BURRITOS

### SERVES 4

*The pork filling is good not only in burritos, but in tacos, tostadas, tortas and tamales as well.*

### INGREDIENTS

900 g/2 lb pork shoulder cut
into cubes

5 large, wide ancho chillies

8 garlic cloves, chopped

¼ tsp oregano, crumbled

½ tsp ground cumin

75 ml/3 fl oz stock

juice of ½ lime

salt and freshly ground black pepper

4 large flour tortillas

simmered pinto beans (see below)

4 Tbsp chopped onion

salsa, to taste

Cover the pork with water and simmer over a low heat for 1 hour or until the water has evaporated and the meat has lightly browned.

Remove the pork from the pan and shred with a fork, tossing it with any juices. Set aside.

Lightly toast the chillies, then remove the stems, seeds and veins. Break or cut them up into small pieces, then place in a saucepan with boiling water to cover. Simmer for 15–20 minutes or until they plump up.

In a blender or food processor, combine the chillies, garlic, oregano, cumin, stock and lime juice until they form a smooth paste.

Heat the meat in its juices and pan drippings, then add the sauce and mix well. Simmer over a low heat for about 20 minutes or until the meat has absorbed the chilli sauce. Season with salt and pepper, and adjust the cumin and oregano to taste.

Warm the tortillas. Into each one, spoon a generous portion of meat, a ladle of beans, then a sprinkling of onion, and salsa to taste. Roll up tightly and serve right away, whilst still hot.

# SIMMERED BEANS

### SERVES 6 ~ 8

*Use these beans as an accompaniment to make* frijoles refritos, *or anywhere it calls for simmered beans. A bowl of warm* frijoles de olla, *along with a few warm tortillas and a chilli or two is the mainstay of the Mexican diet.*

### INGREDIENTS

450 g/1 lb pinto (or pinquito, or pink) or black beans, picked over for stones etc, soaked

2 medium onions, chopped

1 head of garlic, unpeeled and cut
into halves crosswise

225 g/8 oz smoky bacon

several sprigs of mint

salt

Soak the beans in a bowl overnight. Alternatively, place the beans in a saucepan with enough cold water to cover. Bring to the boil, cook for a few minutes, then remove from the heat. Leave, covered, for 1 hour. The beans should have plumped up and softened somewhat, as they will have absorbed the water in the process.

Add the onion, garlic, bacon, mint and water to the pan.

Bring to the boil, then reduce the heat to low and simmer, uncovered, stirring once or twice, for 1½–2 hours or until the beans are softened. Add salt to taste.

# SPICED PORK AND AUBERGINE CHOP SUEY

### SERVES 4

*A spiced, Chinese-style dish of marinated pork and crispy, stir-fried vegetables. Make up your own
vegetable mix, or use prepared stir-fry vegetables from the supermarket if you are in a hurry.
Serve with boiled rice or thread egg noodles.*

### INGREDIENTS

I pork tenderloin, weighing about 450 g/I lb

675 g/I½ lb mixed stir-fry vegetables,
such as celery, carrot, peppers, mange
tout, beansprouts

I aubergine, halved lengthwise and
sliced thinly

4 Tbsp peanut oil

### MARINADE

5-cm/2-inch piece fresh ginger, roughly
grated

I–2 garlic cloves, crushed

I Tbsp five-spice powder

I green chilli, deseeded and very
finely chopped

4 Tbsp soya sauce

I Tbsp chilli sauce

I Tbsp light brown sugar

Trim the pork and cut it into very thin slices. Squeeze the juice from the grated ginger and mix it with the other marinade ingredients, then add the pork and toss the slices in the mixture. Leave to stand for at least I hour, turning occasionally.

Meanwhile, prepare the vegetables for the stir-fry, cutting them all into thin 5-cm/2-inch lengths.

Heat the oil in a wok or large frying pan until almost smoking, then add the pork and the aubergine. Stir-fry for about 4 minutes until both are well browned, then add the remaining vegetables. Continue to cook for a further 2–3 minutes, adding any remaining marinade. Serve the pork dish immediately.

# SAUTÉED LAMB WITH AUBERGINE IN A SAUCE

SERVES 4

## INGREDIENTS

2 large aubergines, ends cut off and thickly sliced

3 Tbsp olive oil

8 lamb cutlets, trimmed

2 garlic cloves, crushed

6 large tomatoes, blanched, skinned and thickly sliced

salt and freshly ground black pepper

1 lemon, sliced, to garnish

sprigs of mint, to garnish

### SAUCE

2 Tbsp chopped fresh mint

150 ml/¼ pint natural yoghurt

freshly ground black pepper

Sprinkle salt over the sliced aubergine and leave for 20 minutes. Rinse the slices and dry with absorbent kitchen paper.

Heat 2 tablespoons of olive oil in a wok or large frying pan over a very high heat and add the lamb cutlets. When the meat is brown, lower the heat and continue to cook until the meat is tender, which will take about 5 minutes on each side. Remove the cutlets from the wok, drain on absorbent kitchen paper, and keep warm in the oven.

Add the remaining oil to the wok and fry the aubergine slices with the garlic until they are lightly browned on both sides. If the oil dries out, add a little more. When the aubergine is cooked, push the slices up the sides of the wok and add the tomato slices. Stir-fry for a few moments and season with salt and pepper.

Make the sauce. Stir the mint into the yoghurt and grind over some black pepper. Serve in a small bowl.

Place the vegetables on a dish and arrange the cutlets over them. Serve garnished with lemon slices and sprigs of fresh mint.

# SHEPHERD'S PIE

SERVES 6

*This dish makes a filling supper and is great for feeding lots of*
*hungry people.*

### INGREDIENTS

675 g/1½ lb potatoes cut into 2.5-cm/
1-inch cubes

2 medium onions, finely chopped

2 garlic cloves, crushed

3 Tbsp olive oil

2 Tbsp tomato purée

150 ml/¼ pint red wine

1 tsp oregano or 2 tsp fresh majoram,
chopped

1 tsp dried basil or 2 tsp finely
chopped fresh basil

2 tsp paprika

1 tsp sugar

salt and freshly ground black pepper

675 g/1½ lb ground beef

50 g/2 oz butter

2 Tbsp single cream

1 Tbsp Parmesan cheese or
2 Tbsp Cheddar cheese

Preheat the oven to 400°F/200°C/
gas 6. Peel the potatoes and cut into
chunks. Boil them in plenty of salted
water for 15 minutes, until tender.

Meanwhile, soften the onions and
garlic in the olive oil over a low heat,
then turn up the heat and add the
tomato purée, wine, herbs, paprika and
sugar, and season with salt and pepper.

Add the beef and cook over a
moderate heat for about 10 minutes,
stirring from time to time, until the
meat loses its pinkness.

Drain the potatoes, season with
plenty of salt and pepper, and mash

well, adding first the butter and then
the cream.

Spread the warm beef in a baking
dish and cover completely with the
mashed potato.

Sprinkle with the cheese and bake
for 20–30 minutes, depending on the
thickness of the meat and potato.

Brown the top under a hot grill.

# ROSEMARY-ROASTED PORK WITH BRAISED MUSHROOMS

### SERVES 6

*Braised mushrooms, Catalan-style, added to the pan juices make a luscious sauce for roasted meat.*
*Most mushrooms are delicious, but you must use fresh tomatoes – canned won't do.*

### INGREDIENTS

1.25 kg/2½ lb boned, lean pork, roasted (rolled, by the butcher, and tied, is excellent and will help it stay tidy during roasting)

several sprigs fresh rosemary

10–12 garlic cloves, half cut into slivers, half chopped

salt and freshly ground black pepper

4 Tbsp olive oil

2 carrots, diced

10 garlic cloves, left whole but peeled

1 large onion, chopped

3 fresh ripe tomatoes, grated and skins discarded

450 g/1 lb mixed fresh wild mushrooms, or cultivated common mushrooms mixed with a few handfuls of dried mixed exotic mushrooms

dry white wine or stock, if needed

Preheat the oven to 350°F/180°C/ gas 4. Make incisions all over the meat. Into each one insert a sprig of rosemary, which you have dipped into a little salt, and a sliver of garlic. Stud the whole roast, then rub it with olive oil.

Scatter the carrots, whole garlic cloves and a few rosemary sprigs on the base of a roasting tin. Place the roast on a roasting rack, if you have one, or on the base of the pan. Place in the oven for 1¼ hours.

Meanwhile, sweat the onion slowly in the remaining olive oil, sprinkling with salt to draw out the juices, until soft, which takes about 20 minutes. Stir in the chopped garlic, then add the tomatoes and raise the heat, cooking until the tomatoes melt into the onions, and the oil begins to separate.

Add the mushrooms, reduce the heat, and cook over medium–low heat, stirring occasionally, until the mushrooms are cooked through. The moisture from the fresh mushrooms should rehydrate any dried ones used, but if they don't, add a little stock or dry white wine to the pan, and boil until the mushrooms rehydrate.

When the mushrooms are tender, season with salt and pepper, and set aside until the meat is ready. (A meat thermometer is useful here so that you can gauge the inside of the meat without cutting into it.)

Remove the cooked pork from its pan, pour off any fat from the surface but save any juices, then add a few tablespoons of wine or stock. Place on the stove and scrape the base of the pan. Add the braised mushrooms and warm through, then set aside and keep warm.

Slice the roast, and serve each portion with a few spoonfuls of the mushroom sauce.

# SHEPHERD'S BUSH CASSOULET

SERVES 6 ~ 8

*The ingredients in this casserole make it into a more interesting variation*
*of this classic method of cooking. As you can prepare it well in advance,*
*it is ideal for feeding large numbers of people.*

## INGREDIENTS

450 g/1 lb white haricot beans

225 g/8 oz piece raw, unsalted bacon

1 bay leaf

225 g/8 oz Toulouse or Polish sausage,
cut into 2.5-cm/1-inch chunks

900 g/2 lb boned shoulder or breast of
lamb cut into 4-cm/1½-inch chunks

seasoned flour

3 Tbsp olive oil

2 medium onions, sliced

4 garlic cloves, crushed

2 Tbsp tomato purée

1 tsp sugar

½ tsp dried thyme

½ tsp dried oregano

300 ml/½ pint red wine

salt and freshly ground black pepper

450 ml/¾ pint stock or water

Preheat the oven to 400°F/200°C/ gas 6. Wash the haricot beans and soak them in cold water overnight.

Change the water, add the bacon and the bay leaf and simmer, covered, for an hour. Drain, discard the bay leaf and cut the bacon into bite-sized chunks. Put the bacon, beans and Toulouse or Polish sausage into a large casserole.

Roll the meat in seasoned flour and brown in oil. Transfer to the casserole.

Fry the onions and garlic in the remains of the oil until they begin to brown. Add the tomato purée, sugar, herbs, wine and plenty of salt and pepper. Simmer for a couple of minutes, then pour into the casserole, together with the stock or water.

Put the casserole, uncovered, into a hot oven for 20 minutes, stirring gently from time to time. Cover the casserole, turn down the heat to 325°F/170°C/gas 3 and cook for a further 2½ hours, stirring occasionally, until the lamb and beans are tender.

You may need to add a little more water, if the casserole looks as if it is getting dry.

# Fresh Chicken with Lemon Grass and Cashew Nuts

SERVES 4

*This delicious main course is surprisingly quick and easy.*
*Serve with a bowl of steaming rice.*

### INGREDIENTS

vegetable oil

2 small dried chillies

1 garlic clove, chopped

450 g/1 lb lean, corn-fed chicken, sliced

½ tsp sugar

1 Tbsp oyster sauce

1 Tbsp Nuoc Mam sauce or
light soya sauce

3 Tbsp chicken stock or water

75 g/3 oz roasted, unsalted cashew nuts

1 Tbsp chopped lemon grass

2 shallots, cut in quarters

With a drop or two of oil, stir-fry the chillies until cooked evenly but not burnt. Set aside.

Stir-fry the garlic with a few more drops of oil until golden. Add the chicken slices, sugar and oyster and Nuoc Mam sauces, and stir-fry until the chicken is golden in colour. Lower the heat and add the stock. Cook for a few more minutes, stirring occasionally.

When the chicken is thoroughly cooked, add the cashew nuts, lemon grass, shallots and chillies, and stir several times, being careful not to break the chillies. Remove from the heat and serve.

# COLD CHICKEN MILLEFOGLIE

SERVES 4 ~ 6

*This cold dish is great for summer parties outdoors. Serve with a selection of your favourite salads and crusty white bread.*

## INGREDIENTS

350 g/12 oz puff pastry

100 ml/4 fl oz Basic Garlic Dressing (page 180)

8–10 canned artichoke hearts, quartered

½ Tbsp oil

1 garlic clove, crushed

1 tsp ground coriander

½ tsp ground cumin

½ tsp turmeric

½ tsp paprika

2 pinches cayenne pepper

1 Tbsp lemon juice

250 ml/8 fl oz stiffly whipped cream

225 g/8 oz cold cooked chicken, cut or torn into bite-sized pieces

salt and freshly ground black pepper

2 Tbsp finely chopped parsley

1 Tbsp mayonnaise or Aïoli (page 171)

Preheat the oven to 450°F/230°C/gas 8. Roll the pastry out thinly and cut into 3 strips, approximately 10 cm/4 inches wide. Prick all over with a fork and bake for 7–10 minutes until well risen and browned. Cool on wire rack until needed. Warm the Basic Garlic Dressing and pour over the artichoke hearts. Set aside for at least 1 hour.

Make the sauce for the chicken. Heat the oil and add to it the garlic, coriander, cumin, turmeric, paprika and cayenne. Stir over a moderate heat for several minutes. Remove from the heat and add the lemon juice, and pour or strain the mixture into the cream. Fold the chicken into the sauce and season with salt and pepper to taste.

To assemble the Millefoglie, put one slice of cooked pastry on a serving dish and spread over it half the chicken mixture. Drain the dressing from the artichoke hearts, mix into them the parsley and put half of this on top of the chicken. Top with the second piece of pastry, the remaining chicken, and the rest of the artichoke mixture.

Spread the underside of the final pastry slice with the mayonnaise or Aïoli and press it gently, sticky side down, onto the artichoke and parsley mixture.

Slice with a very sharp serrated knife and serve immediately.

# CHICKEN MOUSSAKA

SERVES 4 ~ 6

*Moussaka is one of the classic aubergine dishes, and this is one of the best
moussaka recipes ever. Use a covered pan to start the sauce as less oil
is required if the onion is half steamed in its own juices.*

### INGREDIENTS

100 ml/4 fl oz olive oil

2 large onions, chopped

450 g/1 lb boneless chicken, finely diced
or chopped in the food processor

1–2 garlic cloves, crushed

150 ml/¼ pint red wine

400-g/14-oz can chopped tomatoes

2 Tbsp freshly chopped oregano, plus
extra for garnish

salt and freshly ground black pepper

1 Tbsp tomato purée

2 large aubergines, sliced

butter, for greasing

### TOPPING

250 ml/8 fl oz ricotta cheese

100 g/4 oz soft goat's cheese with
garlic and herbs

150 ml/¼ pint natural yoghurt

Heat 2 tablespoons of the oil in a pan, add the onions, cover and cook gently until soft. Remove the lid and stir in the chicken with the garlic. Cook quickly until the chicken changes colour. Add the wine and cook until it has reduced by half. Add all the other ingredients except the aubergines, then simmer slowly for 30–40 minutes, until rich and thick.

Preheat the oven to 425°F/220°C/ gas 7. Add 3–4 tablespoons of the oil to a frying pan. Fry the aubergine slices a few at a time until browned on both sides, adding more oil as necessary. Remove with a slotted spoon and drain on kitchen paper.

Layer the chicken sauce and aubergine slices in a buttered, oven-proof dish, finishing with a layer of aubergine. Make the topping. Blend the cheeses and yoghurt together into a sauce, add salt and pepper to taste, and spoon the mixture over the aubergine. Bake for 25–30 minutes. Serve sprinkled with chopped oregano.

# RED DUCK CURRY

SERVES 6

*This is a very popular dish in Thailand; rich and quite delicious.*

### INGREDIENTS

1.5 l/2¾ pints thin coconut milk

1 roasted duck, boned with skin left on,
cut into 1-cm/½-inch slices

15 cherry tomatoes

5 fresh large red chillies, sliced lengthwise

65 g/2½ oz sweet basil leaves

3 kaffir lime leaves, chopped

3 Tbsp sugar

2 Tbsp fish sauce

1 tsp salt

### RED CURRY PASTE

3 stalks of lemon grass, sliced thinly

65 g/1½ oz chopped galangal (ka)

7 dried red chillies, chopped roughly

3 Tbsp chopped garlic

1 Tbsp shrimp paste

1 tsp chopped kaffir lime leaf

1 tsp chopped coriander root

1 tsp white peppercorns

½ tsp coriander seeds

Pound all the curry paste ingredients together with a mortar and pestle or in a blender to a fine paste.

Heat 2 cups of the coconut milk in a wok or pan, add the curry paste mixture, and cook together for 5 minutes. Add the rest of the coconut milk, bring to the boil, then add the duck, cherry tomatoes and red chilli. Bring back to the boil and then add the rest of the ingredients.

Boil all together for 5 minutes and remove from the heat.

Serve accompanied with rice, salted eggs and sun-dried beef.

# CHICKEN CREOLE

SERVES 6 ~ 8

*This is also a good way of cooking cod steaks – there is no need to fry them first.*

### INGREDIENTS

8 chicken portions

100 g/4 oz peeled prawns

2 Tbsp olive oil

½ tsp dried tarragon

2 garlic cloves, crushed

¼ tsp hot pepper sauce or cayenne

1 large onion, thinly sliced

1 red pepper, cored and thinly sliced

concentrated Tomato Sauce (page 181)

Preheat the oven to 350°F/180°C/ gas 4. Score the chicken pieces and put them in a dish, with the prawns at one end. Pour over them a mixture of the oil, tarragon, garlic and hot pepper sauce or cayenne. Leave to marinate for at least 1 hour before cooking.

Drain the marinade into a frying pan and remove the prawns, keeping to one side until needed.

Fry the chicken in the heated marinade for 7–10 minutes, turning occasionally, until well browned.

Arrange in a roasting tin.

Fry the onion and red pepper in the oil left in the pan until the onion begins to brown, then arrange over the chicken.

Pour the tomato sauce over the vegetables and chicken, cover the pan with foil, and cook for 30 minutes. Remove the foil, increase the heat to 425°F/220°C/gas 7, and bake for another 20 minutes, adding the prawns 5 minutes before serving, to heat them through.

# GARLIC CHICKEN ON A STICK

SERVES 6

*Soak wooden skewers in lemon juice for about 30 minutes before use to stop them from burning.*

### INGREDIENTS

6 chicken breast halves,
skinned and boned

6 garlic cloves, crushed

salt and freshly ground black pepper

freshly squeezed juice of 2 lemons

4 Tbsp olive oil

6 Tbsp finely chopped fresh parsley

Cut the chicken halves into 2.5-cm/ 1-inch pieces and place them in a shallow dish.

In a small bowl, mix together the garlic, salt and freshly ground pepper, lemon juice and olive oil. Pour the marinade over the chicken, stir to coat the meat, cover the dish, and place in the refrigerator for 2–4 hours, turning the chicken and rearranging the pieces from time to time.

Spread the chopped parsley on a serving plate.

Divide the chicken pieces into 6 equal portions, reserving the marinade, and thread the meat on to 6 wooden skewers. Roll each skewer in the chopped parsley to coat evenly.

Arrange the chicken skewers on an oiled grill rack and cook under a preheated grill for 5–10 minutes or until the chicken is golden on the outside and cooked through. Turn and rearrange the skewers, basting with the reserved marinade to add flavour while the meat cooks.

# BOXING DAY MOLE

SERVES 8

*This streamlined version of one of Mexico's most famous national dishes makes a change from the usual methods of dealing with the remains of the Christmas or Thanksgiving turkey and is equally good made with chicken. Serve it with plain boiled rice, refried beans, tortillas and a bowl of Guacamole.*

## INGREDIENTS

turkey bones

1.1 litre/2 pints water

2 medium onions, coarsely chopped

4 garlic cloves, coarsely chopped

salt and freshly ground black pepper

100 g/4 oz canned pimentos, coarsely chopped

1 small red pepper, deseeded and chopped

350 g/12 oz ripe tomatoes, skinned, deseeded and chopped

1 thick slice of white bread, toasted and crumbled

100 g/4 oz ground almonds

50 g/2 oz sesame seeds

2 Tbsp oil or lard

1 tsp ground coriander

½ tsp ground allspice

chilli powder, to taste

2 tsp brown sugar

50 g/2 oz unsweetened chocolate, in small pieces

1 kg/2 lb cold turkey meat, torn into bite-sized pieces

Gently simmer the turkey bones in the water with a third of the onion, a quarter of the garlic and plenty of salt and pepper for 45 minutes, by which time you should have a good stock.

Combine the remaining onion and garlic, pimentos, red pepper, tomatoes, bread, ground almonds, half the sesame seeds and half the turkey stock, and reduce to a smooth purée.

In a large, heavy saucepan, heat the oil or lard, coriander, allspice, chilli powder – you can always add more later if it's not hot enough for you – and sugar, for a couple of minutes.

Add the puréed sauce and stir over a moderate heat for 5 minutes. Add the chocolate and enough stock to dilute the sauce to the thickness of double cream. Season with salt and pepper to taste.

Turn down the heat and cook gently, stirring occasionally, for 10 minutes. Add the turkey and heat for a further 10 minutes.

Toss the remaining sesame seeds over a moderate heat until toasted and sprinkle them over the turkey just before serving.

*Korean Braised Chicken Thighs* ▶

# KOREAN BRAISED CHICKEN THIGHS

SERVES 4

*Chicken thighs become richly flavoured and very tender and succulent when they are steeped*
*in a tasty marinade, then fried and braised in it.*

### INGREDIENTS

8 chicken thighs

4 spring onions, white parts only, very
finely chopped

2.5-cm/1-inch piece of fresh ginger, grated

2 garlic cloves, crushed and chopped

4 Tbsp soya sauce

1 Tbsp sesame oil

1½ Tbsp crushed toasted sesame seeds

2 tsp sugar

vegetable oil for frying

1 red pepper, seeded and diced

2 spring onions, white and pale green
parts, sliced diagonally

Slash each chicken thigh three times and place them in a shallow dish. Mix together the finely chopped spring onions, the ginger, garlic, soya sauce, sesame oil, sesame seeds and sugar. Pour over the chicken. Turn to coat with the sauce and leave in a cool place for about 4 hours, turning occasionally.

Heat a little vegetable oil in a heavy flameproof casserole. Lift the chicken thighs from the marinade, add to the casserole, brown evenly. Pour in the marinade and enough water just to cover the chicken. Bring barely to simmering point. Cover the casserole and leave to cook gently for about 30–35 minutes, turning the chicken occasionally, until very tender.

Add the red pepper and sliced spring onions about 5 minutes before the end of cooking. If necessary, uncover the casserole toward the end of cooking to let the sauce reduce.

# LIVER STROGANOFF

SERVES 4

### INGREDIENTS

450 g/1 lb calves' liver, thinly sliced

1 garlic clove, crushed and juice

1 Tbsp oil

½ tsp fresh bruised sage leaves, chopped

6 black peppercorns, bruised

½ tsp paprika

2 Tbsp dry white wine or dry sherry

225 g/8 oz baby onions

50 g/2 oz butter

25 g/1 oz plain flour

150 ml/¼ pint soured cream

salt and freshly ground black pepper

Cut the liver into strips 0.5 × 5 cm/ ¼ × 2 inch. Pour over them a mixture of the crushed garlic, oil, sage, peppercorns, paprika and wine or sherry, and leave to marinate in a cool place for 2–4 hours, stirring occasionally.

Peel the onions – this is easier if you first loosen the skins by blanching them in boiling water for 30 seconds – and sweat them in the butter, covered, for 10–20 minutes, until they are just tender. Remove the onions from the pan and reserve.

Drain the liver of its marinade, toss it in the flour, and cook in the butter and onion juices for no more than a minute on each side.

Add the garlic juice and onions, and simmer for a minute more. Off the heat, stir in the soured cream, season with salt and pepper to taste, and serve immediately.

# DOUBLE GARLIC CHICKEN

### SERVES 4 ~ 6

*Definitely a dish for garlic lovers. The chicken is flavoured both
inside and out for a full garlic experience.*

## INGREDIENTS

3 heads garlic (about 35 cloves)

1.75–2 kg/3½–4 lb roasting chicken

175 g/6 oz cream cheese or
low-fat soft cheese

1 Tbsp chopped chives

1 Tbsp chopped parsley

salt and freshly ground black pepper

225 g/8 oz green grapes
(seedless and not too sweet)

sprig of rosemary

25 g/1 oz butter

Preheat the oven to 350°F/180°C/ gas 4. Plunge the unpeeled garlic, except for 2 cloves, into a pan of boiling water for 30 seconds, drain, and peel. Boil for a further 2 minutes, drain, and set to one side.

Peel one of the remaining garlic cloves, and cut it in half. Rub the cut side of the garlic over the breast and legs of the chicken, then slice it and its other half.

Peel and crush the last garlic clove and blend it with the cream or low-fat cheese, chives and parsley. Season well with salt and pepper.

Work your fingers under the skin of the chicken breast, carefully freeing it from the meat without tearing it.

Pack the cheese mixture between the loosened skin and the meat, covering the breast completely.

Stuff the body of the chicken with the blanched garlic and the grapes, together with most of the rosemary.

Put the chicken in an oiled roasting pan and tuck slices of garlic and the remaining blades of rosemary between the legs and wings and the body of the chicken.

Sprinkle the breast with salt and dot it with the butter. Cover the breast and feet with foil.

Bake for approximately 1½ hours, until the juice no longer runs pink, removing the foil for the last 20 minutes of cooking to crisp the skin.

# CHICKEN WINGS WITH LIME JUICE AND GARLIC

SERVES 8 ~ 12

*Whenever you buy a whole chicken, freeze the wings if they are not needed. When you have enough collected in the freezer, you can transform them into this deliciously tangy recipe.*

### INGREDIENTS

12 chicken wings

4 garlic cloves, crushed

salt and freshly ground black pepper

freshly squeezed juice of 4 limes

pinch of cayenne pepper

Place the chicken wings in a shallow dish. Rub the crushed garlic all over the chicken wings, then season them with salt and freshly ground black pepper.

Sprinkle the lime juice and cayenne pepper over the chicken wings, cover, and marinate in the refrigerator for 3–4 hours, turning and rearranging them occasionally.

Arrange the chicken wings in a large frying pan and pour the marinade over them. Add just enough cold water to cover the wings and bring quickly to the boil. Cook, uncovered, for 20–25 minutes, or until the chicken is cooked through and the sauce has reduced slightly. Serve warm or, better still, cold the next day.

# CHICKEN WITH PRUNES

SERVES 4

*Prunes make a rich, winey sauce, their sweetness balanced with the spicy, smoky chilli and the tangy edge of tamarind. Serve with boiled potatoes sprinkled with cumin and green onions, or with steamed rice tossed with strips of roasted peeled green peppers and sautéed onions, with a sprinkling of cumin.*

### INGREDIENTS

1 chicken, cut into serving pieces

juice of ½ lime or 4–6 crushed cooked tomatillos

5 garlic cloves, chopped

chipotle salsa or marinade from chipotle chillies, (see Tip page 21) to taste

salt and freshly ground black pepper

flour for dusting

vegetable oil

6–8 tomatoes, diced

1 onion, chopped

100 ml/4 fl oz wine, beer or brandy

300 ml/¼ pint chicken stock

10–12 prunes, stoned

2–3 Tbsp sugar or honey

1 Tbsp tamarind paste or Worcestershire sauce, to taste

½ tsp ground cinnamon

¼ tsp ground allspice or large dash of ground cloves

vinegar

2 Tbsp lightly toasted flaked almonds, to garnish

1 Tbsp chopped fresh coriander, to garnish

Combine the chicken with the lime juice or tomatillos, half the garlic, the chipotle salsa, and salt and pepper. Leave to marinate for 1 hour or better still overnight.

Dust the chicken with flour then lightly brown in oil in a frying pan, taking care it does not burn. Place in a casserole, then pour out the fat from the pan.

Add the tomatoes, onion, wine, beer or brandy, chicken stock and remaining garlic to the pan, and bring to the boil. Simmer for a few minutes until the onion turns translucent, then add the prunes, sugar or honey, tamarind paste or Worcestershire sauce, cinnamon, cloves and chipotle salsa to taste.

Pour the sauce into the casserole, letting it lightly coat the chicken and sink to the bottom of the casserole. Place the prunes under the chicken.

Bake the chicken in a preheated oven at 350°F/180°C/gas 4 for 35–45 minutes or until very tender. Adjust seasoning and serve, sprinkled with toasted almonds and coriander.

# Moroccan Chicken with Lemons and Olives

SERVES 4

*There is little work involved in preparing this dish, which basically simmers away in the oven,*
*and it is never less than delicious.*

### INGREDIENTS

1 chicken, cut into serving pieces

1 Tbsp cumin

2 tsp paprika

½–1 tsp ginger

½–1 tsp turmeric

5 garlic cloves, chopped

several handfuls of fresh coriander, chopped

juice of 2 lemons

black and cayenne pepper, to taste

3–5 Tbsp plain flour

4 tomatoes, chopped (either ripe or canned)

10–15 each (three types in total): green olives of choice, black olives, cracked olives, oil-cured olives, purplish-red olives, Kalamata, pimiento-stuffed green olives, etc., drained

1 lemon, cut into 6 wedges

100 ml/4 fl oz extra-virgin olive oil

250 ml/8 fl oz chicken stock

extra lemon juice, to taste

Preheat the oven to 325°F/170°C/ gas 3. Combine the chicken with the cumin, paprika, ginger, turmeric, garlic, coriander, lemon juice and pepper, and place in a baking dish in a single layer. Leave to marinate for 30 minutes, then add the flour, and toss together to coat well.

Add the tomatoes, olives, lemon wedges, olive oil, and stock to the dish. Bake uncovered for about 1 hour, until the chicken is tender.

# VEGETABLES &
# SALADS

# SAVOURY ROASTED PUMPKIN

### SERVES 4

*Drizzling the pumpkin or squash with olive oil and balsamic vinegar, then baking it,*
*is a simple, healthy way to serve this rich, sweet vegetable.*

### INGREDIENTS

1.25 kg/2 1/2 lb pumpkin, or large orange
squash or other winter squash, cut
into several pieces

3–5 garlic cloves, chopped

3 Tbsp extra-virgin olive oil

1 tsp balsamic vinegar

sea salt and freshly ground black pepper

pinch of mild, red chilli powder

pinch of oregano or sage

Arrange the squash or pumpkin on a baking sheet, and sprinkle all of the other ingredients over it.

Cover tightly with foil, and bake for about an hour at 350°F/180°C/gas 4, or until the pumpkin or squash is tender. Unwrap and serve hot.

### COOK'S TIP

If you have any left-overs these may be mashed with a fork, smoothed with a bit of extra-virgin olive oil, a little chopped garlic, a few drops of lemon, and served as a Mediterranean antipasto or meze-type salad.

# POTATO AND TOMATO GRATIN

### SERVES 4 ~ 6

*This gratin layers potatoes with tomatoes and olive-oil-cooked onions, unlike many other gratins,*
*which are creamy and cheesy. This is terrific warm, but like many dishes cooked in olive oil,*
*it is best served at room temperature the next day.*

### INGREDIENTS

1.25 kg/2½ lb potatoes, preferably waxy
ones, peeled and cut into halves

3–4 onions, thinly sliced

4 Tbsp extra-virgin olive oil

8 garlic cloves, chopped

salt and freshly ground black pepper

400 g/14 oz tomatoes (canned are fine),
coarsely diced or broken up

1 Tbsp chopped fresh oregano

Parboil the potatoes for about 15 minutes, until they are nearly cooked. Remove from the water and leave to cool for about 15 minutes, or until you are able to handle them. Then peel and cut into 3-mm/⅛-inch thick slices.

Meanwhile, fry the onions in a few tablespoons of olive oil, and when they have softened, sprinkle in half the garlic. Season with salt and pepper, and continue to cook until softened and lightly browned.

Layer the onions in the bottom of a 35-cm/14-inch casserole dish, then layer the sliced potatoes and tomatoes, with the remaining garlic, olive oil, salt and pepper, ending with a layer of the tomatoes and a drizzle of olive oil.

Sprinkle with oregano, then bake in a 375°F/190°C/gas 5 oven for 20–30 minutes, or until the top is lightly browned, the whole thing is sizzling, and the potatoes have cooked through.

*Savoury Roasted Pumpkin* ▶

# GARLIC MASH

SERVES 6

*This is particularly good with sausages, steak and roast chicken, or as a nest for baked eggs.*
*Don't count on left-overs, but if there are any they can be chilled, shaped into patties,*
*rolled in flour, and shallow fried in hot fat until brown on both sides.*

### INGREDIENTS

3 heads garlic (about 35 cloves)

100 g/4 oz butter

2 Tbsp plain flour

¼ tsp nutmeg

¼ tsp English mustard

300 ml/½ pint boiling milk

salt and freshly ground black pepper

1 kg/2 lb floury potatoes

3 Tbsp single cream

Separate the garlic cloves and blanch them in boiling water for 1 minute, drain and peel.

Cook them over a low heat, covered, in half the butter for about 20 minutes until tender.

Blend in the flour, nutmeg and mustard, and stir for several minutes without browning.

Remove from the heat and stir in the boiling milk. Season with plenty of salt and pepper.

Return to the pan and simmer for 2 more minutes.

Peel the potatoes and cut into small chunks. Boil for 15 minutes or until just tender and drain. Mash with the remaining butter.

Beat in the reheated garlic purée followed by the cream, one spoonful at a time. The final mixture should not be too runny. Season the mash with salt and pepper to taste and serve immediately.

# OIL-ROASTED ROOT VEGETABLES

SERVES 4

*Root vegetables are delicious when cut into chunks or chips and drenched in olive oil before*
*being roasted to a crispy-brown exterior and a tender, creamy inside.*

### INGREDIENTS

2 of each: carrots, parsnips, potatoes, turnips, celery root, sweet potatoes or any root vegetable you can find

2–3 Tbsp extra-virgin olive oil

salt and freshly ground black pepper

2–3 garlic cloves, chopped

Cut the vegetables into chunks or chips, and blanch them quickly. Drain and toss them in olive oil, salt, and pepper, and arrange on a baking sheet.

Preheat the oven to 400°F/200°C/ gas 6. Roast the vegetables until they are browned and crisp, turning every so soften. Toss them with garlic, and serve.

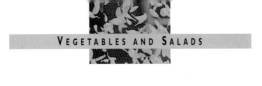

# CHESTNUT HASH

SERVES 4

*Cook the potatoes for this dish in advance or use up any left-over cooked potatoes for speed.*
*Allow the potato to brown on the base of the pan for a crunchier texture.*

### INGREDIENTS

675 g/1½ lb potatoes, peeled and cubed

1 red onion, halved and sliced

50 g/2 oz mange tout

50 g/2 oz broccoli florets

1 courgette, sliced

1 green pepper, deseeded and sliced

75 g/3 oz drained, canned sweetcorn

2 garlic cloves, chopped

1 tsp paprika

2 Tbsp chopped fresh parsley

300 ml/½ pint vegetable oil

50 g/2 oz chestnuts, cooked, peeled
and quartered

freshly ground black pepper

parsley sprigs, to garnish

Cook the potatoes in boiling water
for 20 minutes or until softened.
Drain well and reserve.

Meanwhile, cook the remaining
ingredients in a frying pan for 10
minutes, stirring. Add the drained
potatoes to the pan and cook for a
further 15 minutes, stirring and pressing
down with the back of a spoon. Serve
immediately with crusty bread.

# BUTTER-BRAISED GARLIC

SERVES 3 ~ 4

*Garlic was popular as a vegetable during the Middle Ages, when it was known as 'aquapatys'.*
*It is certainly time that this surprisingly subtle dish had a revival.*

### INGREDIENTS

4 good-sized heads of garlic
(about 60 cloves)

75 g/3 oz butter

salt and freshly ground black pepper

2 Tbsp finely chopped fresh
parsley, to serve

Separate the garlic cloves and simmer in salted water for 15 minutes, until just tender.

Drain, peel carefully, and stew them in the butter over a low heat for a further 5–7 minutes. Season with salt and pepper.

Stir in the chopped parsley and serve over the hot garlic.

# AUBERGINE AND SWEET POTATO CURRY

SERVES 4

*This makes a very substantial main course, but it could also be served as a side dish*
*with meat or fish curries.*

### INGREDIENTS

2 tsp cumin seeds

1 Tbsp mustard seeds

3 Tbsp ghee or sunflower oil

2 small sweet potatoes, about 450 g/1 lb,
peeled and cut into 1-cm/½-inch chunks

1 large onion, finely sliced

2 garlic cloves, finely sliced

1–2 tsp chilli powder

1 tsp ground turmeric

1 large aubergine, cut the same
size as the potato

1 Tbsp poppy seeds

250 ml/8 fl oz water or vegetable stock

2 tsp salt

1 Tbsp torn fresh coriander leaves

Heat a large frying pan over a medium heat, then add the cumin and mustard seeds and dry-fry for 30 seconds or so, until they are aromatic and starting to pop. Transfer to a plate and leave to cool.

Heat the ghee or oil in the pan, add the potatoes and cook for 3–4 minutes until starting to soften. Add the onion, garlic, chilli powder and turmeric and cook for 1–2 minutes, then add the aubergine with the roasted spices and the poppy seeds. Stir in the water or stock and salt, then cover and simmer very slowly for 30–45 minutes until the vegetables are tender.

Season the curry to taste, then serve sprinkled with the coriander.

*Aubergine and Sweet Potato Curry* ▶

# GRATIN OF POTATOES AND MUSHROOMS

SERVES 4

*Soaking the potatoes makes a lighter, less stodgy gratin. If you have no trompettes de la mort,
use porcini, morels or a combination of mixed dried mushrooms.*

## INGREDIENTS

50 g/2 oz trompettes de la mort

250 ml/8 fl oz stock or water

8 baking potatoes

salt and freshly ground black pepper

10 shallots, chopped or sliced

8–10 garlic cloves, chopped

50 g/2 oz butter

300 ml/½ pint single cream

225 g/8 oz grated Parmesan, comte,
fontina, or Gruyère cheese, or a
combination, for sprinkling

1 Tbsp pink peppercorns

2 Tbsp chopped fresh parsley

Place the mushrooms in a saucepan with the stock or water and bring to the boil. Reduce the heat, simmer for 5–10 minutes, or until the mushrooms are tender, then remove them from the heat.

When the mushrooms are cool enough to handle, remove them from the saucepan, and set aside. Strain the mushroom liquid and set aside.

Peel and thinly slice the potatoes, and place them in cold water to cover. Leave for about 30 minutes, then drain, and dry well. Use a clean teatowel and lay the potatoes in it, patting them all dry.

Preheat the oven to 375°F/190°C/gas 5. Butter the base of a gratin dish and place a layer of the potatoes on the base. Sprinkle with salt, pepper, shallot and garlic, and add some little dots of butter, then make another layer of potatoes. Every so often make a layer of the mushrooms. End with the potatoes, dotted with a tablespoon or so of the

butter on the top.

Pour the reserved mushroom liquid over the potatoes, then pour the cream over and finally sprinkle with the cheese.

Bake in the oven for about 1 hour, or until the top is crusty and browned. Serve sprinkled with pink peppercorns and parsley.

# DAL

SERVES 4

### INGREDIENTS

1½ Tbsp ghee or oil

3–4 garlic cloves, crushed

2 tsp turmeric

1 small green chilli, seeded and finely chopped or 2 pinches of chilli powder

2 tsp ground coriander

1 tsp ground cumin

2 medium onions, finely chopped

200 g/7 oz red split lentils

675 ml/1¼ pints water or stock

1 Tbsp tomato purée

½ tsp sugar

salt and freshly ground black pepper

Heat the ghee or oil in a large, heavy pan and fry the garlic and spices for several minutes.

Add the onion, and when it begins to brown, add the lentils.

Pour over the water or stock, add the tomato purée and sugar, and bring to the boil.

Simmer for 40–50 minutes, until the lentils begin to fall apart.

Season with plenty of salt and a little pepper, and serve.

### COOK'S TIP

For a really tasty lentil soup, simply double the quantity of water or stock used, and either sift or blend the cooked Dal.

Dal can also be made with yellow split peas, which must be soaked overnight in a bowl of warm water. Cook the Dal for about 1½ hours, until the peas are tender.

# POTATOES WITH GARLIC, CHEESE AND MILK

SERVES 6

*A filling bake with a crunchy topping, concealing the creamy and tender potatoes underneath.*

### INGREDIENTS

25 g/1 oz butter

2 garlic cloves, crushed

1 kg/2¼ lb potatoes

salt and freshly ground black pepper

nutmeg to taste

1 egg

300 ml/½ pint milk

75 g/3 oz Gruyère cheese, grated

Preheat the oven to 350°F/180°C/ gas 4. Thickly butter a baking dish, then sprinkle in the crushed garlic.

Layer the dish with thin slices of potato cut in rounds, and season with the salt, pepper and nutmeg.

Beat the egg and mix with the milk and pour the mixture over the potatoes so they are all covered.

Sprinkle the grated cheese on top. Bake until the potatoes are tender and the crust is firm and golden.

# WILD MUSHROOM AND CHIPOTLE SALSA

SERVES 4

*The smoky scent of chipotles deliciously sets off the hearty flavour of wild mushrooms. The salsa is delicious with tacos, tostadas and tortillas, or anything from the barbecue.*

### INGREDIENTS

25 g/1 oz dried mushrooms or
175–225 g/6–8 oz fresh mushrooms

½ onion or 3 shallots, chopped

3 garlic cloves, sliced

2–3 Tbsp olive oil

1–2 pinches whole cumin seeds

¼–½ tsp mild chilli powder, such as ancho

4 fresh ripe tomatoes

½ or more chipotle chilli in adobo,
chopped or mashed, or a few shakes of
bottled chipotle

juice of ½ lemon or lime

2 Tbsp chopped fresh coriander

salt, to taste

Rehydrate the dried mushrooms, if using, by either soaking or simmering in hot water until tender. When cool enough to handle, squeeze dry, then chop roughly. You should have about 8 heaped tablespoons of mushrooms. If using fresh mushrooms, clean and chop roughly.

Lightly sauté the onion or shallots and garlic in the olive oil, then sprinkle in the cumin seeds. Add the mushrooms, cook for a few moments, then sprinkle with the chilli powder. Add the tomatoes and cook until reduced to a salsa-like mixture. Then add the chipotle, lemon or lime juice and coriander. Add salt to taste and serve as desired.

# BONANZA BROWN RICE

SERVES 4

*This rice goes very well with chicken.*

### INGREDIENTS

2 garlic cloves, crushed

1 medium onion, finely chopped

½ small red pepper, thinly sliced

2 Tbsp oil

225 g/8 oz brown rice

450 ml/¾ pint canned consommé

250 ml/8 fl oz water

salt and freshly ground black pepper

Sauté the garlic, onion and sweet red pepper in the oil until the onion is transparent and beginning to brown slightly.

Add the rice and cook for several minutes, stirring well.

Pour in the consommé and water, cover the pan, and cook over a low heat for 30–35 minutes, until the rice is just tender. Season with salt and pepper, and serve.

*Wild Mushroom and Chipotle Salsa* ▶

# BROCCOLI WITH GARLIC, HOT PEPPER AND OLIVE OIL

SERVES 4

*This is especially good at room temperature, much like a salad.*

### INGREDIENTS

675 g/1½ lb broccoli raab (a mixture of broccoli and spinach or Swiss chard)

several pinches of hot-pepper flakes

2–3 garlic cloves, chopped

4 Tbsp extra-virgin olive oil

sea salt

juice of ¼–½ lemon

Either steam or blanch the greens, then remove from the pan. Alternatively, you can cook the greens in a covered pan, letting them cook in their own juices.

Place the cooked greens in a pan with the hot-pepper flakes, garlic and olive oil. Cook together, covered, for about 5 minutes.

Season with salt and lemon juice, and let cool. Serve as desired.

# COUNTRY GRILLED AUBERGINE

SERVES 4

*An Italian-style salad of cooked aubergine slices marinated in oil and mint and finished with toasted pine nuts and Parmesan.*

### INGREDIENTS

1 large aubergine, sliced thickly

olive oil, for brushing

50 g/2 oz pine nuts, toasted

2 Tbsp chopped fresh parsley

grated rind of 1 lemon

shaved Parmesan cheese

### MARINADE

100 ml/4 fl oz olive oil

1 garlic clove, crushed

12 large basil leaves, roughly torn

1 Tbsp chopped fresh mint

salt and freshly ground black pepper

1 Tbsp balsamic vinegar

Preheat the grill or griddle pan until very hot, then add the aubergine slices. Brush generously with olive oil, then cook until browned on both sides.

Mix together the ingredients for the marinade in a shallow dish. Add the aubergine slices and turn them in the mixture. Leave for 1–2 hours, then stir in the pine nuts. Serve at room temperature, sprinkled with the parsley, lemon rind and Parmesan, with fresh crusty bread.

# RATATOUILLE

SERVES 4 AS A MAIN COURSE OR 8 AS A STARTER

*This is more of a salad, with the vegetables cooked individually, but it has all the flavours*
*of the classic Mediterranean dish.*

### INGREDIENTS

about 6 Tbsp olive oil

1 large onion, chopped

2 garlic cloves, finely sliced

1 green pepper, cored,
deseeded and sliced

1 courgette, yellow if possible, sliced

1 long thin aubergine, about 5 cm/2 inches
in diameter, cut into 5-mm/¼-inch slices

400-g/14-oz can chopped tomatoes

150 ml/¼ pint red wine

4–5 sprigs fresh thyme

salt and freshly ground black pepper

1 Tbsp freshly torn basil leaves

50 g/2 oz small black stoned olives

225 g/8 oz diced feta cheese

Heat 3 tablespoons of olive oil in a large frying pan, add the onion and cook for about 5 minutes over a medium heat until softened but not brown. Add the garlic and cook for a few seconds longer, then remove the onion and garlic with a slotted spoon and place in a large bowl.

Add the pepper to the pan and cook slowly for 4–5 minutes, then remove with a slotted spoon and place in the bowl with the onion and garlic. Add 1–2 tablespoons of oil to the pan, then add the courgette and cook for 3–4 minutes, turning once.

Remove the courgette with a slotted spoon and add to the bowl.

Add 1 tablespoon of oil to the pan, then add the aubergine slices and fry gently until lightly browned on both sides. Remove the aubergine with a slotted spoon and add to the bowl.

Add the tomatoes to the pan with the red wine and thyme, salt and pepper. Bring to the boil, then simmer gently for 5 minutes. Remove the thyme, then pour the hot sauce over the vegetables in the bowl. Leave to cool, tossing the vegetables in the sauce once or twice.

Just before serving, add the torn basil leaves, olives and cheese. Serve at room temperature for the best flavour.

# CHICORY ORANGE WALNUT SALAD

SERVES 4 ~ 6

### INGREDIENTS

4 plump heads chicory (Belgian endive)

2 large sweet oranges

100 g/4 oz walnut halves

3 Tbsp olive or walnut oil

1 Tbsp lemon juice

1 garlic clove, finely crushed

½ tsp sugar

Cut the chicory into 1-cm/½-inch slices. Peel and slice the oranges – or divide them into segments – removing the skin and pith from each.

Coarsely chop the walnuts, reserving a few for decoration.

Mix the olive or walnut oil, lemon juice, garlic and sugar, and pour this dressing over the combined chicory, orange and walnuts.

Decorate with the reserved walnuts and serve chilled.

# AUBERGINE AND KIDNEY BEAN CHILLI

SERVES 4

*Aubergines make a good alternative to lentils for a vegetable-based chilli sauce. The spicing in this is quite strong – use a little less chilli powder if you prefer. Serve with brown rice or tortilla chips and an avocado dip.*

### INGREDIENTS

3 Tbsp peanut oil

I large onion, chopped

2 tsp chilli powder

I tsp ground cumin

I large aubergine, cut into 1-cm/½-inch chunks

1–2 garlic cloves, crushed

I large cinnamon stick

2 bay leaves

600 ml/1 pint strained tomatoes or thick tomato juice

salt and freshly ground black pepper

350 g/12 oz canned red kidney beans and juice

boiled rice, to serve

soured cream and fresh coriander leaves, to garnish

Heat the oil in a large pan. Add the onion with the chilli powder and cumin and cook for 4–5 minutes over a low heat, until the onion is soft but not browned. It is important to cook the onion slowly so that the spices do not burn.

Add the aubergine and garlic, and cook for 1–2 minutes, then add the cinnamon and bay leaves with the strained tomatoes or tomato juice. Add salt and pepper, then bring to the boil. Cover the pan and simmer the sauce slowly for 10 minutes, then add the kidney beans and their juice. Continue cooking for a further 10 minutes, then remove the cinnamon and bay leaves.

Season the chilli to taste, then serve on a bed of rice with a large spoonful of soured cream, garnished with coriander.

# ARTICHOKES BRAISED WITH HERBS AND OLIVE OIL

SERVES 4 ~ 6

*Artichokes, stuffed with mint, parsley and garlic, then braised with olive oil and lemon, are one of the delights of the Roman kitchen. They make a marvellous antipasto, and left-overs are delicious, too, when added to braised meats, or sliced and served with roasted fish or chicken.*

## INGREDIENTS

4 Tbsp finely chopped parsley

2–3 Tbsp finely chopped, fresh mint leaves, or more as desired

8–10 garlic cloves, finely chopped

salt and freshly ground black pepper

100 ml/ 4 fl oz extra-virgin olive oil

8 medium-sized artichokes

juice of 1 lemon

Preheat the oven to 350°F/180°C/ gas 4. Combine the parsley with the mint, garlic, salt and pepper, and about 3 tablespoons of the olive oil or enough to form a paste. Leave aside to marinate while you prepare the artichokes.

Remove the hard leaves from the artichokes, and cut away the sharp top from the tender, inner leaves. Pull the centre open, and scoop out the thistly inside, using a spoon and a sharp paring knife.

Stuff the inside of each artichoke with the herby mixture, then lay the artichokes in a baking dish in a single layer. Sprinkle with salt, pepper and any left-over herby mixture, then sprinkle with the remaining olive oil and lemon juice, adding enough water to cover the artichokes. Cover with a lid or with aluminium foil.

Bake for about 1 hour. Remove the lid to taste the sauce. If it lacks flavour, pour it into a saucepan and reduce until it condenses and intensifies – you want the liquid to be evaporated to isolate the flavourful oil. Once that has happened, stop boiling immediately. Season with salt, pepper and lemon juice, then pour it back over the artichokes. Serve hot or cold.

# GREEK MUSHROOMS

SERVES 6 ~ 8

*This meze dish is best kept simple, with the use of fresh, firm mushrooms and*
*a good quality olive oil for the best flavour.*

### INGREDIENTS

150 ml/¼ pint olive oil

100 ml/4 fl oz dry white wine

salt and freshly ground black pepper

1 tsp dried thyme

3 garlic cloves, crushed

4 Tbsp chopped fresh parsley

575 g/1¼ lb button mushrooms, cleaned

freshly squeezed juice of 1 lemon

chopped fresh parsley, to garnish

Place all the ingredients, except the mushrooms and half the lemon juice, in a large saucepan and bring to the boil. Reduce the heat and stir in the mushrooms. Cover and simmer for 8–10 minutes.

Transfer the mushrooms and the liquid to a serving dish and allow to cool completely.

Serve at room temperature, sprinkled with the remaining lemon juice and garnished with chopped fresh parsley.

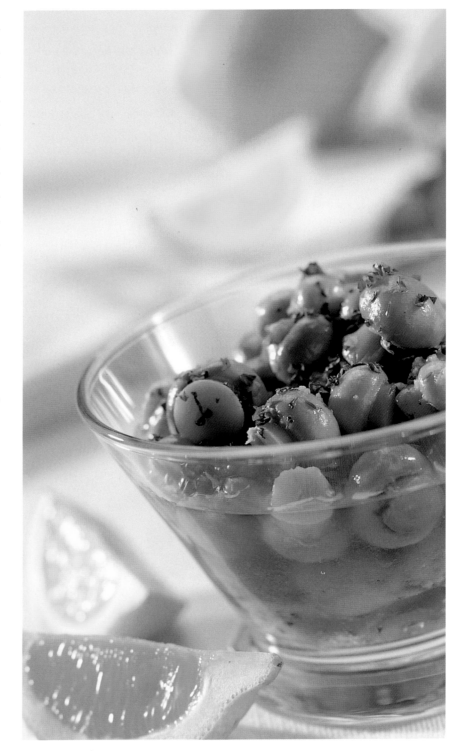

# WILD MUSHROOMS COOKED IN OIL WITH GARLIC

SERVES 4

*This is the classic way to prepare not only porcini, but all sorts of wild mushrooms: simply with extra-virgin olive oil, garlic and parsley. If you like, combine common cultivated mushrooms with dried exotic mushrooms in this recipe.*

### INGREDIENTS

450 g/1 lb porcini, wild or exotic mushrooms, or a combination

3–4 Tbsp extra-virgin olive oil and/or butter

3 garlic cloves, chopped

2 Tbsp chopped fresh parsley

salt and freshly ground black pepper

Clean the mushrooms, taking care to wipe them or trim them of any nasty bits or soggy undersides. Trim off the tough stem ends, and slice the heads and edible stems in half.

Heat the olive oil and/or butter until just threatening to smoke, then throw in the mushrooms, garlic, parsley, salt and pepper. Toss a few times, to coat the mushrooms in the garlicky oil, then reduce the heat to low, cover, and leave the mushrooms to stew very gently in their own juices for about 30 minutes. (This is traditionally done over very low heat, for about 1 hour.)

Serve with chunks of crusty bread.

# HARICOT BEAN SALAD

SERVES 4

### INGREDIENTS

225 g/8 oz dried white haricot beans

175 ml/6 fl oz Basic Garlic Dressing (page 179)

2 garlic cloves, crushed

1 large red pepper, deseeded and thinly sliced

2 small leeks, thinly sliced

1 Tbsp finely chopped spring onions (green part only)

Cover the beans with boiling water and leave to soak overnight. Pour off the soaking water. Cover with fresh water and boil for 1½–2 hours, until tender. You may need to add more water from time to time to prevent them from sticking.

Drain the beans and, while still hot, pour over the Basic Garlic Dressing. Stir in the crushed garlic and cool until needed.

Before serving, stir in the pepper and leeks, and sprinkle with the chopped spring onions.

### COOK'S TIP
Omit the leeks and spring onions, and stir in 2 tablespoons of coarsely chopped fresh mint just before serving.

# SPANISH ROASTED MUSHROOMS

SERVES 4

*This simple Mediterranean dish of roasted mushrooms is sprinkled with fino sherry, garlic and butter,*
*with a scattering of almonds, which toast whilst the mushrooms cook.*

### INGREDIENTS

450 g/1 lb large flat mushrooms

1 Tbsp fino sherry

5 garlic cloves, chopped

40 g/1½ oz butter

1 Tbsp chopped fresh parsley

salt and freshly ground black pepper

3–4 Tbsp flaked almonds

Preheat the oven to 400°F/200°C/ gas 6. Arrange the mushrooms on a large baking sheet and sprinkle the sherry, then the garlic, over the top. Dot with the butter, sprinkle with parsley, salt, pepper and almonds.

Bake in the oven for about 20 minutes, until the mushrooms sizzle and the nuts are toasted. Serve the mushrooms immediately.

# ROASTED OYSTER MUSHROOMS WITH WHOLE GARLIC CLOVES

SERVES 4

*If you prefer, the mushrooms and poached garlic can be sautéed in a large heavy-based frying pan, in several batches, if necessary, so as not to crowd the mushrooms.*

### INGREDIENTS

2 garlic bulbs cloves, separated but unpeeled

450 ml/¾ pints vegetable or chicken stock

450 g/1 lb oyster mushrooms, whole but broken into clumps

75 g/3 oz butter or 6 Tbsp olive oil, or as desired

2 garlic cloves, chopped

several sprigs fresh thyme

1 Tbsp chopped fresh parsley or snipped fresh chives

Preheat the oven to 350°F/180°C/gas 4. Simmer the whole garlic cloves in the stock for about 10 minutes, until almost tender and the liquid has reduced by about half.

Place the mushrooms in a roasting pan. Surround with the garlic cloves and drizzle with the stock. Stud the top of the mushrooms and the garlic cloves with the butter or drizzle with the olive oil, sprinkle with chopped garlic and thyme, then roast for

20–30 minutes. If they are not done, raise the oven temperature to 400°F/200°C/gas 6, and roast for 5–10 minutes more.

Serve sprinkled with chopped parsley or chives.

### COOK'S TIP
Don't throw out the garlic poaching liquid. It is great for making soups or for adding to vegetable or meat stocks to boost the flavour.

# BAKED MIXED VEGETABLES

SERVES 6 ~ 8

*This light and easy-to-prepare dish is a favourite throughout Greece
during spring and summer.*

## INGREDIENTS

6 Tbsp olive oil

3 onions, sliced

675 g/1½ lb small potatoes, peeled and
halved or cut into thick slices

675 g/1½ lb courgettes, cut into chunks

8 ripe tomatoes, peeled and
roughly chopped

2 peppers, deseeded and
sliced into rings

4 garlic cloves, finely chopped

1 tsp dried oregano

4 Tbsp chopped fresh parsley

2 Tbsp chopped fresh dill

salt and freshly ground black pepper

100 ml/4 fl oz water

Preheat the oven to 350°F/180°C/
gas 4. Heat 2 tablespoons of the
olive oil in a frying pan and cook the
onion for 3–5 minutes, until softened but
not coloured. Remove from the heat.

Combine the cooked onion with
the prepared potatoes, courgettes,
tomatoes, peppers, garlic, herbs and
seasoning in a large roasting tin. Add
the water and bake for 1½–2 hours,

until the vegetables are tender and
cooked through, rearranging them
twice during cooking. Serve this dish
warm or cold.

# MIXED VEGETABLE GUMBO

SERVES 4

*Gumbo is a traditional dish of okra and spices from the southern states of America. It usually contains chicken or fish, but make it with just a good selection of vegetables for vegetarian friends.*

## INGREDIENTS

150 ml/¼ pint olive oil, plus extra
if needed

2 large onions, chopped

1 red and 1 green pepper, cored,
deseeded and cut into squares

1 hot chilli, seeded and finely sliced

2 garlic cloves, finely sliced

450 g/1 lb okra, cut into thick slices

400-g/14-oz can chopped tomatoes

25 g/1 oz butter

3 Tbsp flour

2 tsp chilli powder

1 tsp ground cumin

900 ml/1½ pints vegetable stock

4–5 sprigs fresh thyme

salt and freshly ground black pepper

1 aubergine, cut into chunks

1 long, thin aubergine, sliced

Heat 3 tablespoons of oil in a large pan. Add the onion and cook gently until softened but not browned. Add the peppers, hot chilli, garlic and okra. Cook for 5 minutes over a very low heat, then add the tomatoes. Cover and simmer the vegetables for 15 minutes.

Meanwhile, melt the butter in a large flameproof casserole, then add the flour and spices and cook over a low heat until bubbling gently. Remove from the heat and gradually add the stock, then the thyme. Return to the heat and bring slowly to the boil. Simmer the sauce for 1–2 minutes; it should be quite thin, even after boiling. Season well, then add the vegetable mixture. Cover and cook slowly for 30 minutes.

Meanwhile, heat the remaining oil in a large frying pan, add the chopped aubergine and fry until browned, stirring the pieces gently so that they do not break up in the pan. Transfer to the gumbo and simmer for a further 15 minutes.

Add the aubergine slices to the pan and cook on both sides until tender. Season the gumbo and serve garnished with fried aubergine.

# AUBERGINE AND PEPPERS, SZECHUAN-STYLE

SERVES 3 ~ 4

*Szechuan cooking is very spiced. You could serve this as main course by itself, or with a meat or fish dish.*

## INGREDIENTS

peanut oil, for frying

1 large aubergine, cut into 2.5-cm/ 1-inch chunks

2 garlic cloves, crushed

5-cm/2-inch piece fresh ginger, peeled and very finely chopped

1 onion, roughly chopped

2 green peppers, cored, deseeded and cut into 2.5-cm/1-inch pieces

1 red pepper, cored, deseeded and cut into 2.5-cm/1-inch pieces

1 hot red chilli, deseeded and finely shredded

100 ml/4 fl oz well-flavoured vegetable stock

1 Tbsp granulated sugar

1 tsp rice or white wine vinegar

salt and freshly ground black peppers

1 tsp cornflour

1 Tbsp light soya sauce

sesame oil, for sprinkling

Heat 3 tablespoons of oil in a wok. Add the aubergine and stir-fry for 4–5 minutes, until lightly browned. Add more oil if necessary. Remove the aubergine with a slotted spoon and keep warm.

Add a little more oil to the wok, then add the garlic and ginger and fry for just a few seconds before adding the onion and peppers with the chilli.

Stir-fry for 2–3 minutes, then return the aubergine to the wok with the remaining ingredients.

Continue to stir-fry until the sauce has boiled and thickened, at which stage the cornflour will clear. Check the seasoning, adding a little more salt or soya sauce as necessary, then serve immediately, sprinkled with sesame oil, with boiled or fried rice.

# GREEN BEANS WITH CRUSHED GARLIC

SERVES 4

### INGREDIENTS

1 Tbsp vegetable oil

1 onion, finely chopped

4 garlic cloves, finely chopped

3 large green chillies, deseeded and
sliced thinly diagonally

1 tsp ground coriander

½ tsp ground cumin

2 ripe tomatoes, blanched, skinned,
seeded and chopped roughly

450 g/1 lb green beans, washed, trimmed
and halved

½ tsp sugar

pinch of salt

2 Tbsp chopped fresh coriander

Heat the oil in a wok and stir-fry the onion, garlic and green chillies, stirring constantly, for 2 minutes.

Add the coriander and cumin, stir vigorously, and add the chopped tomatoes and beans. Stir and cover the wok for 5 minutes.

Remove the cover, add the sugar and a little salt, and stir again for 1 minute. Add the coriander, stir for 30 seconds, and transfer to a warm serving dish.

**GARLIC GARLIC GARLIC**

# SHIITAKE MUSHROOM, TOFU AND ONION SKEWERS

### SERVES 4

*This makes a good appetizer or a vegetarian main course served on a pile of rice pilaf. It's also delicious served at room temperature, too, so toss some extra on to the barbecue.*

### INGREDIENTS

6–8 fresh shiitake mushrooms, quartered

50 g/2 oz tofu, cut into bite-sized chunks

3–4 onions, cut into bite-sized chunks

5 garlic cloves, chopped

3–5 Tbsp soya sauce

1 Tbsp lime or lemon juice

several shakes of Tabasco sauce

2 Tbsp sesame oil

½ tsp ground cumin

¼ tsp ground coriander

1 Tbsp grated or finely chopped fresh root ginger

several pinches Chinese five-spice powder

3 Tbsp vegetable oil

Soak the bamboo skewers in cold water for 30 minutes; this helps keep them from burning.

Place the shiitake mushrooms, tofu and onions in a shallow, non-metallic pan and sprinkle with the remaining ingredients, turning everything so that it is completely coated with the various flavours. Leave to marinate for at least 30 minutes, preferably overnight, turning several times.

Thread the mushrooms, tofu and onion onto each skewer, then cook over medium heat on the barbecue. Serve hot or at room temperature.

# AUBERGINE AND LENTIL SALAD

SERVES 4

*An excellent winter salad as an alternative to coleslaw – filling and tasty.*

### INGREDIENTS

3 Tbsp sesame seeds

5 Tbsp olive oil

I large onion, finely chopped

I tsp ground cumin

1–2 garlic cloves, crushed

I large aubergine, diced

100 g/4 oz orange lentils

400-g/14-oz can chopped tomatoes

250 ml/8 fl oz vegetable or chicken stock

salt and freshly ground black pepper

I Tbsp freshly chopped mint

Heat a large pan over a medium heat, then add the sesame seeds and dry fry for 2–3 minutes, stirring constantly, until evenly toasted. Transfer to a plate.

Heat 3 tablespoons of the oil in the pan. Add the onion and cumin and cook until starting to brown, then add the garlic and aubergine, and continue to cook for 2–3 minutes. Add the lentils, chopped tomatoes, stock and seasoning. Bring to the boil. Cover and simmer for 30 minutes. Season and leave to cool.

Add the toasted sesame seeds and chopped mint to the mixture, then stir in the remaining olive oil. Cool the salad for about 30 minutes before serving. Do not serve too cold, or the full flavour will be lost.

# PAN-COOKED BLACK MUSHROOMS

SERVES 4

*So simple – a pan of mushrooms is cooked with garlic and olive oil or butter, with nuggets of spring onion, and just enough juices to dip into it with grainy wholemeal bread. This makes a breakfast to wake up to, and a lovely supper, too.*

### INGREDIENTS

450 g/1 lb flat black mushrooms

3–5 garlic cloves, chopped

2 Tbsp olive oil or butter, or more as desired

sea salt

3–4 spring onions, thinly sliced

Place the mushrooms in a large frying pan, black gill sides up, and sprinkle the open caps with the garlic.

Drizzle the olive oil or add the butter to the pan, letting some melt into the pan and brown the mushroom bottoms and some sink into the mushroom gills. When the mushrooms are lightly browned on the skin side, sprinkle with sea salt, turn over, and cook on the other side.

Add the spring onions and continue to cook gently over medium–low heat, until the mushrooms are just tender and slightly juicy. Serve immediately.

### COOK'S TIP

Serve the pan-browned mushrooms and their juices on a bed of broken up fresh naan (or warmed naan or other flat bread), and let the juices soak up into the flat bread. Serve with shavings of Parmesan or pecorino scattered over the top.

# GLAZED GARLIC NEEPS

SERVES 4

*This is very good with most roast meats, particularly beef and ham.*

### INGREDIENTS

2 heads garlic (about 25 cloves), unpeeled

450 g/1 lb young turnips, quartered

150 ml/¼ pint water

50 g/2 oz butter

1½ Tbsp sugar

salt and freshly ground black pepper

1 Tbsp finely chopped parsley, to serve

Separate the garlic cloves. Blanch them in boiling water for 5 minutes, drain and peel.

Put the garlic, turnips, water, butter, sugar and a little salt and pepper into a heavy saucepan and cook gently in a covered pan for about 20 minutes, until the garlic and turnips are tender, but not mushy. If by then the liquid has not evaporated to a syrupy glaze, uncover the pan and quickly boil off the excess.

Check the seasoning and serve, sprinkled with the parsley.

# SAMOSAS

MAKES 12

### INGREDIENTS

50 g/2 oz ghee or butter, melted

1 onion, chopped

1 tsp coriander seeds, ground

1 tsp fresh root ginger, chopped

225 g/8 oz potatoes, boiled and diced but not soft

100 g/4 oz peas

1 tsp garam masala

salt

2 Tbsp water

### PASTRY

225 g/8 oz flour

salt

5 tsp ghee or butter, melted

4 Tbsp natural yoghurt

vegetable oil for frying

Make the filling. Heat the ghee in a frying pan and fry the onions until they are soft. Then add the coriander and ginger.

Add the potatoes and peas, and cook on a low heat for 5 minutes.

Add the garam masala and salt to taste, and cook until all of the moisture has evaporated.

Make the pastry. Sift together the flour and salt and add the melted ghee and yoghurt.

Knead into a soft, smooth dough, cover with a cloth, and leave to stand for 35 minutes.

Knead again and then break up the dough into small round balls.

Roll out each ball on a floured board, making rounds the size of saucers. Cut each round in half.

Moisten the straight edges of the rounds with water and shape them as cones. Place 2 teaspoons of the filling on each half round, moisten the other edges, and seal well.

Deep fry until they are golden.

# AUBERGINE À LA GRECQUE

SERVES 4 ~ 6

*A marinated aubergine salad with mushrooms and chopped parsley. Serve with lots of bread*
*to mop up the delicious juices.*

### INGREDIENTS

1 large aubergine, sliced

about 100 ml/4 fl oz olive oil

salt and freshly ground black pepper

1–2 garlic cloves, crushed

225 g/8 oz white mushrooms, sliced

2–3 Tbsp chopped fresh parsley

Preheat the grill. Arrange the aubergine slices in the pan and brush with olive oil. Grill until browned, turning occasionally.

Place the aubergine slices in a serving dish and add enough oil to moisten, but not so much that they are swimming in it. Season well, add the garlic, mushrooms and parsley and stir gently. Leave in the refrigerator for 1–2 hours, then serve at room temperature for best flavour.

# WARM CHICKEN LIVER SALAD WITH GARLIC CROUTONS

SERVES 4 ~ 6

### INGREDIENTS

3 Tbsp olive oil

2 garlic cloves, crushed

1 Cos or iceberg lettuce torn into
bite-sized pieces

225 g/8 oz fresh young spinach leaves,
torn into bite-sized pieces

6 strips streaky bacon, cut
into 1-cm/½-inch pieces

350 g/12 oz chicken livers

3 slices white bread cut into
1-cm/½-inch cubes

2 tsp sugar

1 Tbsp Garlic Vinegar (page 169)
or wine vinegar

1 Tbsp finely chopped chives

Put the oil and garlic into a frying pan and leave to infuse. Combine the lettuce and spinach in a salad bowl or in individual serving bowls and then leave to one side.

In another pan, fry the bacon until crisp, drain on absorbent kitchen paper and keep warm.

Fry the chicken livers in the bacon fat for about 5 minutes or until firm and well browned on the outside, but still slightly pink in the middle. Drain and keep warm.

Fry the bread cubes in the garlicky oil until golden and crisp. Drain and keep warm.

Heat the bacon fat, and add the sugar and vinegar. Cook gently until the sugar dissolves.

Arrange the chicken livers and bacon on top of the lettuce and spinach. Pour over the warm dressing, and serve immediately, topped with the garlic croutons and chives.

# WHITE HARICOT BEANS WITH GARLIC AND TOMATO

SERVES 4

### INGREDIENTS

450 g/1 lb dried haricot beans

4 garlic cloves

100 g/4 oz onions

50 g/2 oz butter

150 ml/¼ pint tomato purée

salt and freshly ground black pepper

Soak the dried beans in cold water for 2 hours. Drain.

Crush the garlic cloves and roughly slice the onion. Soften them in the butter over a low heat.

Stir in the drained beans, the tomato purée and enough water to cover the beans by 2.5 cm/1 inch or

so. Bring the mixture to the boil, then lower the heat to a gentle simmer. (Check the water level during cooking and top up to the original level halfway through if necessary.)

Season to taste with salt and pepper when the beans are tender.

# EASTERN PASTA SALAD

SERVES 4 ~ 6

*A traditional combination of mint and lemon makes this dish a salad for summer. Choose your favourite pasta shapes, and serve with warm pitta bread to mop up the delicious dressing.*

### INGREDIENTS

350 g/12 oz dried pasta

dash of olive oil

400-g/14-oz can chickpeas, drained

4 Tbsp fresh mint, chopped

finely grated rind of 1 lemon

### DRESSING

3 garlic cloves, crushed

6 Tbsp extra-virgin olive oil

3 Tbsp white wine vinegar

freshly squeezed juice of 1 lemon

salt and freshly ground black pepper

Bring a large saucepan of water to the boil, and add the pasta with a dash of olive oil. Cook for about 10 minutes, stirring occasionally, until tender. Drain and rinse under cold running water. Drain again, and place in a large mixing bowl.

Add the chickpeas, mint, and lemon rind to the pasta. Place all the dressing ingredients in a screw-top jar, and shake well to mix. Pour the dressing over the bean mixture and mix well to combine. Cover, and chill for at least 30 minutes. Toss before serving.

# PRESERVES, SAUCES & DIPS

# AUBERGINES PRESERVED WITH MINT

MAKES ABOUT 2 KG/4¼ LB

*Try to use preserving jars for this recipe, as they make excellent presents. The aubergines must remain completely covered by the oil to be properly preserved.*

### INGREDIENTS

1 kg/2¼ lb small aubergines

salt

600 ml/1 pint white wine vinegar

6–8 garlic cloves, according to size, finely sliced

50 g/2 oz fresh mint leaves, left whole

1 Tbsp mixed peppercorns

2 large green chillies, deseeded and finely sliced

450 ml/¾ pint fruity olive oil

Cut the aubergines into quarters lengthwise, then into 5-cm/2-inch chunks. Layer them in a colander with plenty of salt. Leave to stand for 2–3 hours, or overnight. Rinse thoroughly, then drain and shake dry.

Bring the vinegar to the boil in a deep pan, then add the aubergines and garlic and boil for 5 minutes. Stir once or twice, to keep the aubergines covered with the vinegar. Drain and allow to cool completely.

Layer the aubergines and garlic alternately with the mint in warm, clean preserving jars. Season each layer with a mixture of the peppercorns and sliced chillies, and pack the layers tightly by pressing down firmly with a wooden spoon.

Pour half the oil into the jars, to just cover the aubergines, then cover and leave overnight. By the next day, the aubergines will have absorbed much of the oil. Add sufficient extra oil to cover the aubergines completely, then seal the jars and leave for at least a week before serving.

# GARLIC HONEY

MAKES 675 G/1½ LB

*This is a useful addition to salad dressings and marinades, and for glazing pork and chicken before roasting. It is also a traditional remedy for coughs, cold sores and acne – and hard-core garlic fanciers.*

### INGREDIENTS

30 garlic cloves, peeled

675 g/1½ lb clear honey

Put the garlic cloves in a large, screw-top jar, and pour the honey over them. There should be about 2.5 cm/1 inch between the honey and the top of the jar.

Cover the jar tightly and leave in a warm place for at least 1 week, turning upside down occasionally.

The juices released by the garlic will begin to turn the honey syrupy, and the goodness – and the flavour – of the garlic will pass to the honey.

◀ *Aubergines Preserved with Mint*

# AUBERGINE CREAM

SERVES 6 ~ 8

*Sometimes called* Hünkâr Begendi *or Sultan's Delight, this delicate creamy dish is served as a sauce for meat or fish, or as a dip.*

### INGREDIENTS

2 large aubergines

1 Tbsp lemon juice

2 garlic cloves, finely chopped

50 g/2 oz butter

40 g/1½ oz flour

450 ml/¾ pint milk

salt and freshly ground black pepper

75 g/3 oz freshly grated Parmesan

chopped fresh parsley, to garnish

Cook the aubergines on the barbecue, under the grill, or in a hot oven until the skins are wrinkled and blistered and the flesh is tender, turning once or twice. Cover with a damp cloth and leave to stand for 10–15 minutes, then peel off the skin. Leave the aubergine flesh in a bowl of cold water with the lemon juice until required, to prevent discolouration.

Melt the butter in a large pan and add the garlic, then remove from the heat and stir in the flour. Cook slowly over a low heat for about 2 minutes, then put the pan to one side. Drain the aubergine and squeeze dry with your hands. Add to the pan and blend either with a potato masher or with a hand-held blender. Gradually stir in the milk.

Bring the sauce slowly to the boil over a low heat, then season to taste. Simmer the sauce for about 15 minutes, or until it no longer tastes floury. Stir in the cheese, then season again if necessary.

Pour into a warm bowl or dish and sprinkle with chopped parsley.

# SESAME SEED AND GARLIC MAYONNAISE

MAKES ABOUT 350 ML/12 FL OZ

*Note that raw eggs used in this recipe should not be consumed by people with weak immune systems or pregnant women.*

### INGREDIENTS

2 egg yolks

2 garlic cloves

salt

2 tsp white rice vinegar

250 ml/8 fl oz mild olive oil (or half olive oil and half peanut oil)

2 chopped spring onions

1 Tbsp sesame seeds, roasted

freshly ground black pepper

Put the egg yolks, garlic, salt and vinegar into a blender or food processor. Mix together briefly. With the motor running, slowly trickle in the olive oil. Add the spring onions almost at the end.

Transfer to a bowl. Fold in the sesame seeds and season the mixture with black pepper.

*Aubergine Cream* ▶

# COCONUT MARINADE

MAKES ABOUT 250 ML/8 FL OZ

*This Asian-style marinade works well with firm fish, such as monkfish,*

*or with chicken, turkey, pork or lamb.*

### INGREDIENTS

150 ml/¼ pint boiling water

75 g/3 oz creamed coconut

1 tsp lime juice

1 shallot, finely chopped

1 garlic clove, finely chopped

1 lemon grass stalk, thoroughly crushed

seeds from 3 cardamom pods, crushed

1-cm/½-inch piece of fresh ginger, grated

½ tsp ground cumin

freshly ground black pepper

Pour the boiling water over the coconut and stir until smooth. Add the remaining ingredients and allow to cool before using.

# GARLIC CHILLI PEPPER JELLY

MAKES ABOUT 1.75 KG/4 LB

*This is a very good relish to serve with roasts and cold meat.*

### INGREDIENTS

1¾ kg/4 lb cooking apples

2 heads garlic (about 25 cloves)

10 small chilli peppers

1 litre/2 pints water

preserving sugar

Cut the apples into 2.5-cm/1-inch chunks, but do not peel or core them. Separate and peel the garlic cloves, and cut each in half lengthwise. Halve the chilli peppers.

Put the apples, garlic and chilli peppers into a preserving pan with the water, and stew for about 1 hour, until the apples are reduced to pulp. Tip into a jelly bag, or thick cloth, and leave to drain overnight. Do not be tempted to speed up the flow of juice by squeezing the bag, because this will only make the juice cloudy.

Measure the juice into a clean pan with 225 g/8 oz of sugar for every 600 ml/1 pint of liquid. Stir over a gentle heat until the sugar has completely dissolved. Boil rapidly for 10 minutes, until a little of the jelly sets when cooled on a plate, and wrinkles when you push it with your finger.

While the jelly is still hot, pour into dry, warmed jars, filling them almost to the brim. Cover the surface of the jelly with a disc of waxed paper. Put a cellophane or waxed paper cover over each jar, secure with thin string or a rubber band, and store in a dark, cool, dry place until ready to use.

# GARLIC VINEGAR

MAKES 600 ML/1 PINT

*This vinegar is very handy for salad dressings and marinades for fish, chicken and seafood.*

### INGREDIENTS

8–10 garlic cloves

coarse salt

600 ml/1 pint white wine or tarragon vinegar

Crush the garlic finely with the salt, and put the mixture into a large, heat-proof jar.

Bring the vinegar to the boil and pour over the garlic.

Allow to cool and then cover. Leave to infuse for 2–3 weeks.

Strain and bottle for use.

### COOK'S TIP

Red Wine Garlic Vinegar – for use in strongly flavoured marinades like those for stewing beef, pot roasts, and game – is made by saving red wine bottle ends and letting them 'turn'. Use 10 cloves of garlic to 600 ml/ 1 pint of the liquid, and warm the vinegar until hand hot before pouring it over the crushed garlic.

# ROAST TOMATO AND GARLIC VINAIGRETTE

MAKES ABOUT 250 ML/8 FL OZ

*Pour the dressing over grilled red peppers, courgettes, aubergines and onions, or toss with pasta.*

### INGREDIENTS

1 large tomato

3 plump garlic cloves, unpeeled

1 tsp sherry vinegar

4 Tbsp virgin olive oil

salt and freshly ground black pepper

Preheat the grill. Grill the tomato and garlic until softened, charred and blistered. Allow them both to cool, then peel them. Seed and chop the tomato.

Put the garlic and tomato into a blender or food processor and mix until smooth.

Add the vinegar then, with the motor running, slowly pour in the oil until well emulsified. Season to taste.

# AÏOLI

MAKES ABOUT 600 ML/1 PINT

*Aïoli is simply the ultimate garlic sauce. Although originally served with prawns, it is sensational on anything from hamburgers to Bouillabaisse. Note that the raw eggs used in this recipe should not be consumed by people with weak immune systems and pregnant women.*

### INGREDIENTS

4–6 garlic cloves (though of course you can use more)

pinch of salt

3 egg yolks

450 ml/¾ pint olive oil

lemon juice to taste

water or single cream (optional)

Chop the garlic finely and pound in a mortar with the salt until smooth. Beat in the egg yolks.

Add the oil, drop by drop at first, then in a thin stream once the mixture is glossy and beginning to thicken.

Add lemon juice to taste, and if it is too solid for your liking, add a little water or single cream.

To stop a skin forming on the Aïoli, cover with a piece of plastic film that touches the surface.

### COOK'S TIP

For Almond Skordalia, add 1 tablespoon each of fresh white breadcrumbs, ground almonds and chopped parsley and a pinch of cayenne to each cup of Aïoli, and flavour with lemon or lime juice to taste. This sauce is traditionally served with cold, cooked vegetables. For Aïoli Verde, add to each cup of Aïoli a handful of parsley, 2–3 sprigs of fresh tarragon, 2–3 sprigs of fresh chervil and ½ handful of spinach, which have been simmered together in salted water until tender, drained and sieved or blended to a smooth purée.

◀ *Roast Tomato and Garlic Vinaigrette*

# SKORDALIA

SERVES 4

*This Greek-style garlic sauce is as much about olive oil as it is about garlic. It is actually a mayonnaise, but does not use eggs to emulsify it. Skordalia is eaten with all sorts of vegetables, crisp fish, either fried or barbecued and hard-boiled eggs.*

### INGREDIENTS

2–3 large garlic cloves

large pinch of salt

juice of ½ lemon, or more to taste

1 small, freshly boiled and tender, peeled potato, broken into several pieces, plus a few Tbsp of its cooking water

100 ml/4 fl oz extra-virgin olive oil, or as needed

Using a mortar and pestle, crush the garlic with the salt until it forms a paste, then work in the lemon juice. Mix until it forms a smooth and creamy texture.

Work in the potato and its cooking water, then slowly work in the olive oil, starting with a tablespoon or so, and repeat until the sauce is rich and delicious. After a while, you can add a slightly larger amount at a time, and stir it in with a fork or spoon.

# PISTOU

SERVES 4

*Unlike pesto, pistou does not have a thickening made with crushed nuts, but, like pesto,*
*it is often enriched with grated, sharp, Parmesan cheese. Stir pistou into pasta, steamed vegetables*
*or a Mediterranean-style vegetable soup.*

### INGREDIENTS

3 garlic cloves, peeled

several handfuls of fresh, sweet-basil
leaves, torn coarsely

5 Tbsp extra-virgin olive oil or
more, as needed

6 Tbsp grated Parmesan, or to taste

Crush the garlic with a mortar and
pestle, then transfer it to a food
processor or blender, and continue to
crush it more finely.

Add the basil, then slowly add the
olive oil, working the mixture in until it
forms a smooth paste. Add enough
olive oil for it to be smooth and oily,
then stir in the cheese.

Store the pistou in a bowl or jar
with a layer of olive oil over the top,
for no longer than 2 weeks. If you
wish to store it longer, you can freeze
it for up to 4 months, but omit the
cheese when freezing to ensure that it
remains fresh.

# AUBERGINE PESTO

SERVES 4

*A relatively low-fat pesto with a hint of smokiness from the aubergine. If fresh basil is unavailable,*
*try mixing 1 teaspoon of dried basil into chopped fresh parsley instead.*

### INGREDIENTS

1 large aubergine

1 large handful of fresh basil leaves

2–3 garlic cloves, roughly chopped

65 g/2½ oz pine nuts

75 g/3 oz freshly grated Parmesan cheese

1 tsp coarse sea salt

4 Tbsp olive oil

Parmesan shavings and basil
sprigs, to garnish

Cook the aubergine over a barbecue, under a grill, or in a hot oven until the skin is wrinkled and blistered and the flesh is tender. Leave to cool slightly for about 10 minutes, then peel off the skin.

Blend all the remaining ingredients in a blender or food processor, then add the aubergine and blend again. Garnish with Parmesan and basil.

# MARINARA SAUCE

SERVES 4-6

*This quantity of sauce is enough for 450 g/1 lb of pasta. Traditionally, it is served without cheese,*
*but if you must, use a strong hard cheese such as Parmesan or pecorino.*

### INGREDIENTS

2 medium onions, thinly sliced

2 garlic cloves, crushed

2 Tbsp olive oil

400-g/14-oz can of tomatoes

1 Tbsp tomato purée

1 tsp sugar

1 tsp dried oregano

1 tsp paprika

salt and freshly ground black pepper

Fry the onions and garlic in the oil until they brown slightly. Lower the heat and continue to cook for 15–20 minutes, until soft.

Add the tomatoes, tomato purée, sugar, oregano and paprika. Cook rapidly for about 10 minutes, until the tomatoes break down.

Add salt and pepper to taste, and serve with pasta.

### COOK'S TIP

Stir 10 stoned black olives and 2 tablespoons of drained finely chopped anchovy fillets to the finished sauce and heat through for a few moments before serving.

# RÉMOULADE SAUCE

MAKES ABOUT 250 ML/8 FL OZ

*Traditionally this sauce is mixed with cold cooked prawns and served over lettuce with various garnishes such as tomatoes and olives, but it can also be used as a seafood dip.*

### INGREDIENTS

1 Tbsp olive oil

100 ml/4 fl oz mayonnaise

2 Tbsp soured cream

1 hard-boiled egg, shelled and finely chopped

1 Tbsp capers, drained and chopped

1 garlic clove, crushed

1 Tbsp finely chopped fresh parsley

2 chopped spring onions

2 Tbsp ketchup

1 tsp lemon juice

1 Tbsp Creole mustard

½ tsp prepared horseradish

¼ tsp cayenne

¼ tsp salt

few drops of Tabasco sauce

In a medium bowl, whisk the olive oil into the mayonnaise until it is all absorbed. Add the remaining ingredients and whisk until smooth. Check the seasoning and adjust, then chill for several hours or overnight to let the flavours blend.

# PESTO

SERVES 4–6

*Although Pesto is traditionally served as a sauce for pasta, it goes well with cold meats,*
*grilled fish, in soup, or on salads with a little extra oil and a dash of lemon juice.*

### INGREDIENTS

40 g/1½ oz finely chopped fresh
basil leaves

2 Tbsp pine kernels

50 g/2 oz Parmesan cheese, finely grated,
or half Parmesan and half sardo cheese

3 garlic cloves, finely chopped

6 Tbsp olive oil

Combine the basil, pine kernels, cheese and garlic in a blender or food processor, and reduce to a thick, green, aromatic paste.

Add the oil, a little at a time, until well incorporated.

### COOK'S TIP

For Walnut Pesto, replace half the olive oil with walnut oil and use chopped walnuts instead of the pine kernels used in this recipe.

# UNCOOKED SALSA WITH GARLIC AND TOMATO

SERVES 4

*This is a classic salsa, rich with garlic, parsley and coriander. For a chunky salsa, leave it as it is;*
*for a smooth purée, give it a whirl in the blender for a moment or two.*

### INGREDIENTS

3 garlic cloves, chopped

2 jalapeño or serrano chillies, chopped

½ onion, chopped

450 g/1 lb flavourful raw tomatoes,
chopped

2–3 Tbsp chopped fresh parsley

2–3 Tbsp chopped fresh coriander

salt and ground cumin, to taste

juice of 1 lime

Combine all the ingredients and taste for seasoning. It will keep for 4–5 days in the refrigerator.

# YOGHURT, CUCUMBER AND GARLIC DIP

SERVES 4 ~ 6

*This light and refreshing dip should always be served well chilled.*

### INGREDIENTS

450 g/1 lb natural yoghurt

½ cucumber

3 garlic cloves, crushed

2 Tbsp chopped fresh mint

2 Tbsp olive oil

1 Tbsp white wine vinegar

salt

Place the yoghurt in a medium-sized bowl. Peel and grate the cucumber, squeezing a little at a time in the palm of your hand to remove the excess water. Stir the cucumber into the yoghurt.

Stir in the garlic, most of the fresh mint, olive oil and vinegar. Season with salt. Cover and chill in the refrigerator until required. Just before serving, garnish with remaining mint.

# SALSA VERDE

SERVES 4-6

*Green and piquant, this sauce of fresh herbs is excellent with any fish, hot or cold, and it goes well with hard-boiled eggs. Since it is so very good with prawns, why not try it in a seafood cocktail?*

### INGREDIENTS

3 garlic cloves, finely chopped

50 g/2 oz finely chopped parsley

1 Tbsp finely chopped watercress leaves

1 Tbsp mixed fresh herbs, finely chopped (basil, marjoram and a little thyme, sage, chervil and dill)

coarse salt

4 Tbsp olive oil

juice of 1–2 lemons

1–2 tsp sugar

freshly ground black pepper

Blend or pound together in a mortar, the garlic, parsley, watercress, fresh mixed herbs and a little coarse salt, until they form a smooth paste.

Add the oil, a spoonful at a time, and mix well after each addition. Add the lemon juice and season with sugar, salt and pepper to taste.

# VINEGAR-BASED SAUCE

MAKES 350 ML/12 FL OZ

*In São Paulo, this sauce is used to marinate the meats in and then after cooking it is used as an accompaniment to the meal.*

## INGREDIENTS

2 onions, chopped very finely

3 garlic cloves, chopped very finely

3 tomatoes, peeled, deseeded and chopped very finely

¼ tsp sugar

6 Tbsp chopped fresh parsley

4 Tbsp chopped fresh coriander

250 ml/8 fl oz white wine vinegar

salt and freshly ground black pepper

Combine all the ingredients, with salt and pepper to taste. Serve in a small bowl, so people help themselves.

Set aside or store in the refrigerator before serving to allow the flavours to penetrate.

# GARLIC BUTTER

## INGREDIENTS

100 g/4 oz butter, softened

3–6 garlic cloves, unpeeled

salt and freshly ground black pepper

Cream the butter. Blanch the garlic in boiling water for 1 minute, drain and peel. Crush the garlic to a fine paste with a pinch of salt and mix in the butter. Season and chill.

## VARIATIONS

**Parsley Garlic Butter**

Add 1½ tablespoon of chopped fresh parsley.

**Herb and Garlic Butter**

Add 1½ tablespoon of chopped fresh mixed herbs.

**Mustard Garlic Butter**

Add 1 tablespoon of mild French mustard.

**Chilli Garlic Butter**

Add chilli powder to taste and 2 teaspoons of tomato purée.

# CLARIFIED GARLIC BUTTER

MAKES 100 G/4 OZ

*This butter can be used for frying, especially potatoes, and can be brushed over pastry before baking, and over cooked buns and bagels before heating. It is also particularly good with vegetables, such as asparagus and artichokes.*

### INGREDIENTS

3–6 garlic cloves, unpeeled

100 g/4 oz butter

salt and freshly ground black pepper

Blanch the unpeeled garlic in boiling water for 1 minute. Drain and peel them.

Slice the garlic, and heat gently for 5 minutes in the butter with a little salt and pepper to season.

Skim the butter and strain it through a piece of muslin or a very fine sieve. Keep covered in the fridge until needed.

# BASIC GARLIC DRESSING

SERVES 4 ~ 6

*A basic garlic dressing makes an interesting change from a normal vinaigrette. It is best served with a crisp, fresh salad, but goes equally well in cold pasta for a quick and easy supper dish. For variations to the basic ingredients, see the Cook's Tip below.*

### INGREDIENTS

1–2 garlic cloves, crushed

1 tsp sugar

2 Tbsp wine vinegar or Garlic Vinegar (page 169)

6 Tbsp olive oil

salt and freshly ground black pepper

Combine all the ingredients in a screw-top jar, cover and shake well. Adjust seasoning before serving.

If you like, add fresh or dried herbs to taste depending on what you are serving the dressing with.

### COOK'S TIP

Replace the oil with soured cream or yoghurt, and the vinegar with lemon juice (the cream version is excellent with 1 tablespoon of freshly grated horseradish added to it).

Add 1 teaspoon of mild French mustard. This dressing is especially good served over warm green beans as a first course.

# COOKED TOMATO SAUCE

MAKES 2 LITRES/3½ PINTS

*This tomato and pepper sauce can be served with grilled fish or thinned with stock for soup.*

### INGREDIENTS

2 tsp cumin seeds

1.5 kg/3 lb fresh or canned tomatoes, diced

6 Tbsp vegetable oil

2–3 small to medium-sized onions, peeled and chopped

4–6 garlic cloves, chopped

1 Tbsp dried oregano, crumbled

2–3 small hot dried chillies, crumbled, or 1 large mild green chilli, roasted, skinned and diced

1 green pepper, roasted, skinned and diced

salt

2–4 Tbsp chopped fresh coriander (optional)

Toast the cumin seeds in an ungreased, heavy-based pan until fragrant, then crush coarsely. Set aside. Purée the tomatoes and set aside.

In the oil, fry the onions and garlic until softened, then add the cumin seeds, oregano, chillies, green pepper and puréed tomatoes.

Simmer, stirring often, for about 45 minutes or until the sauce is richly flavoured and thickened. Season with salt to taste and add coriander if wished.

# CONCENTRATED TOMATO SAUCE

*This rich sauce can be served with pasta as it is, or with mince and liquid added. It is delicious poured over chicken pieces or fish steaks before baking, or used to top homemade pizza. It will also flavour soups and stews, and it is an excellent relish for cold meats, hamburgers and frankfurters.*

### INGREDIENTS

2 medium onions, finely chopped

2–3 garlic cloves, crushed

2 Tbsp olive oil

3 Tbsp tomato purée

3 Tbsp wine or water

1 tsp dried oregano

1 tsp paprika

1 tsp sugar

salt and freshly ground black pepper

Fry the onions and garlic in the oil until they begin to brown. Turn down the heat and simmer, covered, for 10–15 minutes or until softened.

Add the tomato purée, wine or water, oregano, paprika and sugar.

Season with salt and pepper to taste.

Allow the sauce to bubble for 5 minutes, stirring constantly, and then serve.

# DRINKS & DESSERTS

# LHASSI WITH A BANG

SERVES 2

*Traditionally served with hot food to soothe the palate, this version*
*will take your guests by surprise!*

### INGREDIENTS

300 ml/½ pint Greek yoghurt

100 ml/¼ pint iced water

1 large garlic clove, finely chopped

pinch of salt

1 Tbsp coarsely chopped fresh mint

sprigs of mint, to serve

Stir the ingredients together. Serve in two chilled, old-fashioned glasses, garnished with sprigs of mint.

# GARLIC BLOODSHOT

SERVES 4 ~ 6

*A cross between a Bloody Mary and a Bullshot, this is recommended*
*for Sunday brunch or a hangover.*

### INGREDIENTS

175 ml/6 fl oz vodka

175 ml/6 fl oz chilled consommé or
beef stock

300 ml/½ pint chilled tomato juice

3 tsp garlic juice

1 tsp sugar

juice of half a lemon

1 tsp Worcestershire sauce

salt and cayenne pepper

Stir the ingredients together in a glass jug. Season with salt and cayenne pepper to taste, and serve poured over ice in tall glasses.

# GARLIC MULL

SERVES 4 ~ 6

*This is a marvellously warming drink to serve on a chilly evening. Keep the saucepan*
*on the go and top up your glass when you are ready for the next one!*

### INGREDIENTS

1 bottle robust red wine

½ lemon, thickly sliced

small orange, stuck with 6 cloves

1 Tbsp brown sugar

7.5-cm/3-inch piece of stick cinnamon,
bruised

6 unpeeled cloves of garlic, bruised

glass of port or brandy (optional)

little grated nutmeg, to serve

Heat all the ingredients very slowly in a large, heavy saucepan to just below boiling point. Use equal quantities of water and wine if you want the drink to go further.

Strain into mugs or thick glasses and top with a pinch of grated nutmeg.

# MARGARITA MIA

SERVES 2

*Adding garlic to this classic drink gives it an interesting twist.*

### INGREDIENTS

½ garlic clove

salt

4 Tbsp tequila

1½ Tbsp fresh lime juice

2 tsp Cointreau

crushed ice

Bruise the garlic and rub the cut side of the clove round the rims of two standard 90 g/3½ oz cocktail glasses.

Dip the rims of the glasses in salt and chill them in the refrigerator.

Shake the tequila, lime juice and Cointreau together with ice in a screw-top jar and strain – so that the ice doesn't dilute the drink – into the prepared glasses.

# GARLIC VODKA

MAKES 600 ML/1 PINT

*Kick-start the evening with this powerful drink, and continue the theme by serving a garlic-filled dinner.*

### INGREDIENTS

75 g/3 oz garlic cloves

600 ml/1 pint vodka

1 Tbsp sugar

Blanch the unpeeled garlic cloves in boiling water for 30 seconds. Drain them and then prick each clove several times.

Put the garlic cloves into an empty wine bottle, add the sugar and pour over the vodka. Cork securely and leave for 2–3 months. Taste a little and, if not sufficiently garlicky, leave aside for a little longer.

When the desired strength is reached, drain and rebottle. This will now keep indefinitely.

### COOK'S TIP

Garlic Brandy can be made in the same way, but for Garlic Gin double the quantity of sugar.
A few strips of thinly peeled orange rind make a good addition.

*Margarita Mia* ▶

# LIME AND GARLIC GRANITÉ

SERVES 6

*On its own, this frozen ice is refreshing between courses and renews the palate*

*for the next taste sensation on the menu.*

### INGREDIENTS

600 ml/1 pint water

100 g/4 oz sugar

3 garlic cloves, quartered

300 ml/½ pint freshly squeezed
lime juice

rind of a lime, finely grated (optional)

twists of lime peel, to serve

Boil the water, sugar and garlic together for 5 minutes. Strain and set aside to cool.

Stir in the lime juice and grated lime peel (if used), and freeze, stirring from time to time, until granular but still slightly mushy.

Decorate with twists of lime peel, and serve with thin shortbread or *langues de chat.*

# GREEN FRUIT SALAD

SERVES 4

*Fresh green fruit salad is an ideal ending to a summer barbecue feast.*
*For a change, the sweet flavours are mingled with a hint of garlic,*
*coming from the glossy honey.*

## INGREDIENTS

1 large, ripe pear

175 g/6 oz seedless green grapes

1 small lime, skinned and segmented

2 kiwi fruit, peeled and sliced

2 Tbsp Garlic Honey (page 165)

2 tsp lime or lemon juice

1 Tbsp kirsch or tequila (optional)

1 tsp finely chopped fresh mint, to serve

Quarter the unpeeled pear, remove the core, and cut the quarters across in 5 mm/¼-inch slices.

Combine the pear slices with the grapes, lime and sliced kiwi fruit.

Mix the Garlic Honey with the lime or lemon juice, and the kirsch or tequila. Pour over the fruit and chill.

Sprinkle with mint, and serve accompanied with single cream or plain yoghurt.

# GARLIC FUDGE

SERVES 4-6

*The deliciously buttery taste of this classic sweet is given an unexpected bite with the addition of garlic. The strong and savoury flavour it imparts actually helps to take away some of the sweetness, so if you normally find fudge to be too saccharine, have a go at this, you'll be hooked in no time!*

### INGREDIENTS

50 g/2 oz butter

6 garlic cloves, peeled and halved

250 ml/8 fl oz evaporated milk

450 g/1 lb granulated sugar

pinch of salt

Put the butter, garlic, evaporated milk, sugar and salt into a large heavy pan and cook over a very low heat for 10–15 minutes, stirring occasionally, until the sugar no longer 'crunches' under the spoon.

Remove the garlic. Bring the mixture to a slow, rolling boil, stirring it continuously.

Keep the mixture bubbling, stirring frequently, until it thickens and becomes a darker gold in colour.

Test for readiness by cooling a drop of the mixture in a saucer of cold water; when it stays together cleanly and does not cloud the water, take the pan off the heat and leave to stand for 5 minutes.

Beat the fudge vigorously until it begins to crystallize on the sides of the pan.

Spread the fudge about 1 cm/ ½ inch thick in a foil-lined tray. When firm but still warm, score with a wet knife into 2.5-cm/1-inch squares. Leave to cool, and store in waxed paper or a plastic bag in an airtight container. This fudge is best eaten within the week.

# INDEX